THE WAR OF 1812

Past Justifications
and Present Interpretations

Problems in American Civilization

UNDER THE EDITORIAL DIRECTION OF *George Rogers Taylor*

THE WAR OF 1812
Past Justifications
and Present Interpretations

EDITED WITH AN INTRODUCTION BY
George Rogers Taylor

Problems in American Civilization

D. C. HEATH AND COMPANY: Boston

ENGLEWOOD · INDIANAPOLIS · DALLAS · SAN FRANCISCO · ATLANTA

INTRODUCTION

IN commenting on the entry of the United States into the War of 1812 Henry Adams wrote: "A less competent administrative system seldom drifted, by reason of its incompetence, into war with a superior enemy."[1] Yet in his multi-volume biography of James Madison, Irving Brant pictures Madison as a strong executive who, despite having to deal with a narrowly partisan and at times disloyal opposition, led the United States into a second war for independence.[2] The foregoing illustrate but one of the many differences in viewpoint which confront the student who seeks to understand the involvement of the United States in the War of 1812, a war which from beginning to end presents a series of puzzles and paradoxes. Its causes were unclear at the time and remain to this day the subject of lively dispute. The conduct of the war on land proved almost incredibly incompetent and blundering. And the conflict ended in a treaty of peace which failed to mention the chief issues which were alleged to have contributed to its beginning.

The readings in Part I of this volume provide materials from the contemporary debate: The report of The Select Committee on Foreign Relations, excerpts from speeches in the Twelfth Congress, and President Madison's war message of June 1, 1812. The student is urged to study and analyze these documents and speeches before reading further—to weigh the evidence for himself before

consulting the interpretative essays.

The great debate over entry into the war took place to a large extent in the House of Representatives rather than in the United States Senate. The House was at the time the great public forum. Its proceedings were printed more completely than were those of the Senate. Henry Clay had resigned from the Senate and taken over the speakership of the House in order to head The War Hawks, the leaders of the war party in that more important branch of the national legislature. The reader will note that all of the speeches reproduced in these readings have been taken from the proceedings of the House of Representatives. Moreover, the leaders whose speeches are included represented the Frontier or the South Atlantic States. From these two regions came not only the leading War Hawks, but their most vocal and effective opposition. The most articulate opponents of the war were dissident Republicans, men like John Randolph of Virginia and Richard Stanford of North Carolina. The Federalists also strongly opposed entry into the war and the speech by Daniel Sheffey from western Virginia provides an illustration of Federalist oratory. The main voting strength of the Federalists lay, of course, principally in the more northern states. But, for the most part, the members of this opposition did not participate in the debate. A minority party, disagreeing among themselves and without strong leaders, they sulked and plotted in their tents.

The provocations which contemporaries emphasized as causing the demand for war are easily identified from the

[1] Henry Adams, *History of the United States of America* (New York: Charles Scribner's Sons, 1890), V, 163.

[2] Irving Brant, *James Madison, The President 1809–1812* (Indianapolis: The Bobbs-Merrill Company, Inc., 1956).

readings included in Part I. Briefly summarized they are: 1) British violation of American rights of uninterrupted commerce on the high seas, 2) Impressment of seamen, 3) Arming and incitement of Indians on the frontier, 4) The desire of Americans to annex Canada and Florida, 5) Belief that British measures were responsible for depressing the prices of southern staples with resulting economic depression, and 6) Insults to national honor and self-respect. Though these supposed causes are readily established, the attempt to evaluate them raises a host of questions. Is the reasoning logical and consistent? Are the arguments plausible? Are they pertinent? Are the declared motives the real ones or are they presented merely to sway public opinion?

The very names which have sometimes been given to this war—the Second War for Independence, the War for Maritime Rights, Mr. Madison's War, or simply The War of 1812—indicate a certain amount of disagreement as to the relative importance of the various causes alleged for the war. In Part II of this volume, this disagreement is further exemplified. The reader will note that the authors whose studies appear are aware that they are not presenting a complete or definitive analysis, yet each is emphasizing an aspect which he considers of crucial importance. It is not the intention here to evaluate the arguments presented. That is the student's task. Some questions, however, may help him to read these authors critically—and perhaps encourage him to pursue his inquiries further.

If the war was fought to establish maritime rights or to secure American sailors from impressment, why did the most insistent demand for war come from the noncommercial South and those frontier areas most distant from the sea? And why did the strongest opposition center in the three southern New England states and in such northern ports as Boston, Providence, and New York? Was the war fought because of fear of the Indians and a belief that the British were inciting them against the U.S.? But had not Harrison provoked the Indians to battle and defeated them at Tippecanoe in the autumn of 1811? And were they not so weak in relative numbers, equipment, and organization that they were being pushed back on all parts of the frontier and their lands seized through treaties which were being forced upon them? What evidence is there that the British were provoking Indian hostility or that the British were not more interested in peace than war along their long border with the United States? Or was the real incentive a war of conquest which would add Canada and Florida to United States territory? And, in any case, if either of these motives was significant to frontiersmen, how do they explain the overwhelming support of the war by the citizens of areas remote from the frontier such as North and South Carolina and Pennsylvania?

What of the contention that falling prices and economic depression in western and southern states led the people living there to demand war because they held the British responsible? Were British commercial restrictions really an important factor? And in any case, surely this does not account for pro-war sentiment in Maryland and Pennsylvania—states from which large shipments of grain and provisions to the Spanish Peninsula were bringing high prices and rising incomes. Or was the basic cause of the war the patriotic resentment of a people who had been too long insulted by Great Britain—of Americans, who according to Norman K. Risjord, "had a belly full" and could take no more? But of what did they have a "belly full"? Insults on the high seas? British-provoked Indian atrocities? Commercial restraints which brought economic depression? And why did the insults offend the patriotic ardor of the people in Lexington, Virginia, Charleston, South Carolina, and Harrisburg, Pennsylvania, but not that of the proud citizens of Staunton, Virginia, Trenton, New Jersey, or Springfield, Massachusetts?

If the student pursues these questions, as well as others which will surely occur to him as he reads the interpretations developed in this volume, he may find some difficulty in evaluating the major causes of the War of 1812. Yet he should not be discouraged if he does not easily solve this complex puzzle. He will at least gain some appreciation of the difficulty of understanding and interpreting the American past. He may also discover the satisfaction and excitement which comes from putting his mind to work on an unsolved problem.

CONTENTS

CHRONOLOGY

Events Leading to the War of 1812

May 16, 1806	The British decree a blockade of the European coast from Brest to the Elbe River.
November 21, 1806	Napoleon's Berlin Decree declares the British Isles in a state of blockade.
January 7, 1807	British Order in Council bars all shipping from coastal trade of France and her allies.
June 22, 1807	U. S. frigate *Chesapeake* is fired upon by British frigate *Leopard* and forced to permit removal of four of crew claimed to be British deserters.
December 17, 1807	Napoleon's Milan Decree declares all vessels obeying the British Orders in Council or searched by the British subject to seizure and confiscation as British property.
December 22, 1807	U. S. Embargo Act forbids virtually all commerce with foreign countries.
March 1, 1809	Non-Intercourse Act repeals Embargo Act, effective March 15, reopens trade with all nations save France and Great Britain, and provides for resumption of trade with either of the two countries named should it cease violating neutral rights.
May 1, 1810	Macon's Bill No. 2 provides that with expiration of the Non-Intercourse Act, commerce be reopened with Great Britain and France. But if one of these nations revokes its restrictive measures, then non-intercourse may be revived against the other.
November 2, 1810	President Madison accepts French claim that their edicts have been revoked.
February 2, 1811	President Madison revives the non-intercourse law against Great Britain.
May 16, 1811	The U. S. frigate *President*, cruising off Sandy Hook to prevent impressment of American sailors by the British, pursues and disables the British Corvette *Little Belt*.
November 4, 1811	Opening of the Twelfth Congress of the United States.
November 7–8, 1811	William Henry Harrison defeats the Indians under Tecumseh in the Battle of Tippecanoe.
April 4, 1812	A general embargo regarded as a prelude to war is imposed.
June 18, 1812	War declared on Great Britain.

THE CLASH OF ISSUES

A widely accepted explanation for the War of 1812 is presented by Julius W. Pratt:

The belief that the United States would one day annex Canada had a continuous existence from the early days of the War of Independence to the War of 1812. . . . The rise of Tecumseh, backed, as was universally believed, by the British, produced an urgent demand in the Northwest that the British be expelled from Canada. This demand was a factor of primary importance in bringing on the war.

But A. L. Burt questions this interpretation and reverts to an older and more conventional view:

In the President's historic message of June 1, 1812, recommending a declaration of war, Britain is charged most positively with "a series of acts, hostile to the United States as an independent and neutral nation," and after the enumeration of these acts, which are a catalogue of the maritime grievances, a short paragraph insinuating that there was some connection between the hostility of the savages and their intercourse with the British is inserted as a sort of afterthought. This is the only reference to the Indian troubles, and it makes no definite charge. Apparently the administration did not consider the native hostilities to be a cause of war any more than did the majority in Congress.

Emphasis on economic motives has as its most recent sponsor Margaret Kinard Latimer:

[The Westerners] began to become painfully aware of foreign restrictions on American commerce, and to these they directed more and more blame for their economic ills. . . . In 1812, "The right of exporting the productions of our own soil and industry to foreign markets" seemed as real to the hemp and tobacco growers of Kentucky as to the large-scale cotton producers of South Carolina. . . . The new generation of the Republican party, with an aim to protect and promote the direct commerce of the country that seemed more Federalist than Jeffersonian, was strongly spearheaded by men from the South and Southwest who worked together successfully in a Congressional drive for war.

Norman K. Risjord objects, stressing psychological considerations:

The modern tendency to seek materialistic motives and economic factors in all human relations has greatly obscured one of the basic causes of the War of 1812. . . . A casual search through the letters and speeches of contemporaries reveals that those who fought the war were primarily concerned with the honor and integrity of the nation.

And Henry Adams has his own unique point of view:

The experiment of thrusting the country into war to inflame it, as crude ore might be thrown into a furnace, was avowed by the party leaders, from President Madison downward, and was in truth the only excuse for a course otherwise resembling an attempt at suicide. Many nations have gone to war in pure gayety of heart; but perhaps the United States were first to force themselves into a war they dreaded, in the hope that the war itself might create the spirit they lacked.

I. THE CAUSES OF WAR AS SEEN IN 1811–1812

The Report of the Committee on Foreign Relations of the United States House of Representatives, November 29, 1811.

WITHOUT recurring . . . to the multiplied wrongs of partial or temporary operation, of which we have so just cause of complaint against the two great belligerents, your committee will only call your attention, at this time, to the systematic aggression of those Powers, authorized by their edicts against neutral commerce—a system, which, as regarded its principles, was founded on pretensions that went to the subversion of our national independence; and which, although now abandoned by one Power, is, in its broad and destructive operation, as still enforced by the other, sapping the foundation of our prosperity.

It is more than five years since England and France, in violation of those principles of justice and public law, held sacred by all civilized nations, commenced this unprecedented system by seizing the property of the citizens of the United States, peaceably pursuing their lawful commerce on the high seas. To shield themselves from the odium which such outrage must incur, each of the belligerents sought a pretext in the conduct of the other—each attempting to justify his system of rapine as a retaliation for similar acts on the part of his enemy. As if the law of nations, founded on the eternal rules of justice, could sanction a principle, which, if ingrafted into our municipal code, would excuse the crime of one robber, upon the sole plea that the unfortunate object of his rapacity was also a victim to the injustice of another. The fact of priority could be true as to one only of the parties, and whether true or false, could furnish no ground of justification.

The United States thus unexpectedly and violently assailed by the two greatest Powers in Europe, withdrew their citizens and property from the ocean: and cherishing the blessing of peace, although the occasion would have fully justified war, sought redress in an appeal to the justice and magnanimity of the belligerents. When this appeal had failed of the success which was due to its moderation, other measures, founded on the same pacific policy, but applying to the interests instead of the justice of the belligerents, were resorted to. Such was the character of the non-intercourse and non-importation laws, which invited the return of both Powers to their former state of amicable relations, by offering commercial advantages to the one who should first revoke his hostile edicts, and imposing restrictions on the other.

France, at length, availing herself of the proffers made equally to her and her enemy, by the non-importation law of May, 1810, announced the repeal, on the

Annals of the Congress of the United States, 12th Congress, 1st Session, Part I (Washington: Gales and Seaton, 1853), cols. 374–77. Referred to hereafter as *Annals of Congress.* All references are to this volume.

first of the following November, of the decrees of Berlin and Milan. And it affords a subject of sincere congratulation to be informed, through the official organs of the Government, that those decrees are, so far at least as our rights are concerned, really and practically at an end.

It was confidently expected, that this act on the part of France would have been immediately followed by a revocation on the part of Great Britain of her Orders in Council. If our reliance on her justice had been impaired by the wrongs she had inflicted, yet, when she had plighted her faith to the world that the sole motive of her aggression on neutral commerce was to be found in the Berlin and Milan decrees, we looked forward to the extinction of those decrees, as the period when the freedom of the seas would be again restored. In this reasonable expectation we have, however, been disappointed. A year has elapsed since the French decrees were rescinded, and yet Great Britain, instead of retracing *pari passu* that course of unjustifiable attack on neutral rights, in which she professed to be only the reluctant follower of France, has advanced with bolder and continually increasing strides. To the categorical demands lately made by our Government for the repeal of her Orders in Council, she has affected to deny the practical extinction of the French decrees, and she has, moreover, advanced a new and unexpected demand, increasing in hostility the orders themselves. She has insisted, through her accredited Minister at this place, that the repeal of the Orders in Council must be preceded, not only by the practical abandonment of the decrees of Berlin and Milan, so far as they infringe the neutral rights of the United States; but by the renunciation

on the part of France, of the whole of her system of commercial warfare against Great Britain, of which those decrees originally formed a part.

This system is understood to consist in a course of measures adopted by France and the other Powers on the Continent subject to, or in alliance with her, calculated to prevent the introduction into their territories of the produce and manufactures of Great Britain and her colonies; and to annihilate her trade with them. However hostile these regulations may be on the part of France towards Great Britain, or however sensibly the latter may feel their effects, they are, nevertheless, to be regarded only as the expedients of one enemy against another, for which the United States, as a neutral Power, can, in no respect, be responsible; they are, too, in exact conformity with those which Great Britain has herself adopted and acted upon in time of peace as well as war. And it is not to be presumed that France would yield to the unauthorized demand of America what she seems to have considered as one of the most powerful engines of the present war.

Such are the pretensions upon which Great Britain founds the violation of the maritime rights of the United States—pretensions not theoretical merely, but followed up by a desolating war upon our unprotected commerce. The ships of the United States, laden with the products of our own soil and labor, navigated by our own citizens, and peaceably pursuing a lawful trade, are seized on our own coasts, at the very mouths of our harbors, condemned and confiscated.

Your committee are not, however, of that sect whose worship is at the shrine of a calculating avarice. And while we are laying before you the just complaints of our merchants against the plunder of their ships and cargoes, we cannot refrain from presenting to the justice and humanity of our country the unhappy case of our impressed seamen. Although the groans of these victims of barbarity for the loss of (what should be dearer to Americans than life) their liberty; although the cries of their wives and children in the privation of protectors and parents, have, of late, been drowned in the louder clamors at the loss of property; yet is the practice of forcing our mariners into the British navy, in violation of the rights of our flag, carried on with unabated rigor and severity. If it be our duty to encourage the fair and legitimate commerce of this country by protecting the property of the merchant; then, indeed, by as much as life and liberty are more estimable than ships and goods, so much more impressive is the duty to shield the persons of our seamen, whose hard and honest services are employed equally with those of the merchants in advancing, under the mantle of its laws, the interests of their country.

To sum up, in a word, the great causes of complaint against Great Britain, your committee need only say, that the United States, as a sovereign and independent Power, claim the right to use the ocean, which is the common and acknowledged highway of nations, for the purposes of transporting, in their own vessels, the products of their own soil and the acquisitions of their own industry, to a market in the ports of friendly nations, and to bring home, in return, such articles as their necessities or convenience may require—always regarding the rights of belligerents, as defined by the established laws of nations. Great Britain, in defiance of this incontestable right, captures every American vessel bound to, or re-

turning from, a port where her commerce is not favored; enslaves our seamen, and in spite of our remonstrances, perseveres in these aggressions.

To wrongs so daring in character, and so disgraceful in their execution, it is impossible that the people of the United States should remain indifferent. We must now tamely and quietly submit, or we must resist by those means which God has placed within our reach.

Your committee would not cast a shade over the American name by the expression of a doubt which branch of this alternative will be embraced. The occasion is now presented when the national character, misunderstood and traduced for a time by foreign and domestic enemies, should be vindicated. If we have not rushed to the field of battle like the nations who are led by the mad ambition of a single chief, or the avarice of a corrupted court, it has not proceeded from a fear of war, but from our love of justice and humanity. That proud spirit of liberty and independence which sustained our fathers in the successful assertion of their rights against foreign aggression is not yet sunk. The patriotic fire of the Revolution still burns in the American breast with a holy and unextinguishable flame, and will conduct this nation to those high destinies which are not less the reward of dignified moderation than of exalted valor.

But we have borne with injury until forbearance has ceased to be a virtue. The sovereignty and independence of these States, purchased and sanctified by the blood of our fathers, from whom we received them, not for ourselves only, but as the inheritance of our posterity, are deliberately and systematically violated. And the period has arrived, when, in the opinion of your committee, it is the sacred duty of Congress to call forth the patriotism and resources of the country. By the aid of these, and with the blessing of God, we confidently trust we shall be enabled to procure that redress which has been sought for by justice, by remonstrance, and forbearance, in vain.

Your committee, reserving for a future report those ulterior measures, which, in their opinion, ought to be pursued, would, at this time, earnestly recommend, in the words of the President, "that the United States be put into an armor and attitude demanded by the crisis, and corresponding with the national spirit and expectations."

The Debate in the Twelfth Congress

Selections from speeches made in the United States House of Representatives during the sessions of the Twelfth Congress.

DEFENSE OF THE COMMITTEE'S REPORT
(1) Peter B. Porter

Porter, a Republican from Buffalo, New York, served as Chairman of the House Committee on Foreign Relations. He was a member of both the Eleventh and the Twelfth Congresses.

THE committee, Mr. P. said, after examining the various documents accompanying the President's Message, were satisfied, as he presumed every member of the House was, that all hopes of accommodating our differences with Great Britain by negotiation must be abandoned. When they looked at the correspondence between the two Governments; when they observed the miserable shifts and evasions (for they were entitled to no better appellation) to which Great Britain resorted to excuse the violations of our maritime rights, it was impossible not to perceive that her conduct towards us was not regulated even by her own sense of justice, but solely by a regard to the probable extent of our forbearance. The last six years had been marked by a series of progressive encroachments on our rights; and the principles by which she publicly upheld her aggressions, were as mutable as her conduct. We had seen her one year advancing doctrines, which the year before she had reprobated. We had seen her one day capturing our vessels under pretexts, which on the preceding day she would have been ashamed or afraid to avow. Indeed, said Mr. P., she seems to have been constantly and carefully feeling our pulse, to ascertain what potions we would bear; and if we go on submitting to one indignity after another, it will not be long before we shall see British subjects, not only taking our property in our harbors, but trampling on our persons in the streets of our cities.

Having become convinced that all hopes from further negotiation were idle, the committee, Mr. P. said, were led to the consideration of another question, which was—whether the maritime rights which Great Britain is violating were such as we ought to support at the hazard and expense of a war. And he believed he was correct in stating that the committee was unanimously of the opinion that they were. The committee thought that the Orders in Council, so far as they go to interrupt our direct trade, that is, the carrying of the productions of this country to a market in the ports of friendly nations, and returning with the proceeds of them—ought to be resisted by war. How far we ought to go in support of what is commonly called the carrying trade, although the question was agitated in the committee, no definitive opinion was expressed. It was not deemed necessary, at this time, to express such an opinion, inasmuch as the injury we sustain by the inhibition of this trade is merged in the greater one to our direct trade.

The Orders in Council, Mr. P. said, of which there seemed now to be no prospect of a speedy repeal—certainly none during the continuance of the present war—authorized the capture of our vessels bound to and from ports where British commerce is not favorably received; and as that nation is at war with most of the civilized world, the effect was (as he understood from those who had much better information on the subject than he could pretend to) to cut up, at once, about three-fourths of our best and most profitable commerce. It was impossible that the mercantile or agricultural interests of the United States, which on the

question of a right to the direct trade could never be separated, could submit to such impositions. It was his opinion, that going upon the ground of a mere pecuniary calculation, a calculation of profits and loss, it would be for our interest to go to war to remove the Orders in Council, rather than submit to them, even during the term of their probable continuance.

But there was another point of view in which the subject presented itself to the committee, and that was as regarded the character of the country. We were a young nation, and he hoped we cherished a little pride and spirit, as well as a great deal of justice and moderation. Our situation was not unlike that of a young man just entering into life, and who, if he tamely submitted to one cool, deliberate, intentional indignity, might safely calculate to be kicked and cuffed for the whole of the remainder of his life; or, if he should afterwards undertake to retrieve his character, must do it at ten times the expense which it would have cost him at first to support it. We should clearly understand and define those rights which as a nation we ought to support, and we should support them at every hazard. If there be any such thing as rights between nations surely the people of the United States, occupying the half of a continent, have a right to navigate the seas, without being molested by the inhabitants of the little island of Great Britain.

It was under these views of the subject that the committee did not hesitate to give it as their opinion that we ought to go to war in opposition to the Orders in Council.

(2) Felix Grundy

After holding important public offices in his home state of Tennessee,
Grundy was elected to the Twelfth Congress. He was an ardent Republi-
can and one of those most impatient for war with Britain.

IT is not the carrying trade, properly so called, about which this nation and Great Britain are at present contending. Were this the only question now under consideration, I should feel great unwillingness (however clear our claim might be) to involve the nation in war, for the assertion of a right, in the enjoyment of which the community at large are not more deeply concerned. The true question in controversy, is of a very different character; it involves the interest of the whole nation: It is the right of exporting the productions of our own soil and industry to foreign markets. Sir, our vessels are now captured when destined to the ports of France, and condemned by the British Courts of Admiralty, without even the pretext of having on board contraband of war, enemies' property, or, having in any other respect violated the laws of nations. These depredations on our lawful commerce, under whatever ostensible pretence committed, are not to be traced to any maxims or rules of public law, but to the maritime supremacy, and pride of the British nation. This hostile and unjust policy of that country towards us, is not to be wondered at, when we recollect that the United States are already the second commercial nation in the world. The rapid growth of our commercial importance, has not only awakened the jealousy of the commercial interests of Great Britain, but her statesmen, no doubt, anticipate with deep concern, the maritime greatness of this Republic.

The unjust and unprecedented demands now made by Great Britain, that we shall cause the markets of the Continent to be opened to her manufactures, fully justifies the views I have suggested.

That we as a neutral nation should interfere between belligerents in their municipal regulations, will not be contended for by any one. From the course pursued by that nation for some years past, it evidently appears, that neither public law nor justice, but power alone, is made by her the test of maritime rights.

What, Mr. Speaker, are we now called on to decide? It is, whether we will resist by force the attempt, made by that Government, to subject our maritime rights to the arbitrary and capricious rule of her will; for my part I am not prepared to say that this country shall submit to have her commerce interdicted or regulated, by any foreign nation. Sir, I prefer war to submission.

Over and above these unjust pretensions of the British Government, for many years past they have been in the practice of impressing our seamen, from merchant vessels; this unjust and lawless invasion of personal liberty, calls loudly for the interposition of this Government. To those better acquainted with the facts in relation to it, I leave it to fill up the picture. My mind is irresistibly drawn to the West.

Although others may not strongly feel the bearing which the late transactions in that quarter have on this subject, upon my mind they have great influence. It

Annals of Congress, 424–27.

cannot be believed by any man who will reflect, that the savage tribes, uninfluenced by other Powers, would think of making war on the United States. They understand too well their own weakness, and our strength. They have already felt the weight of our arms; they know they hold the very soil on which they live as tenants at sufferance. How, then, sir, are we to account for their late conduct? In one way only; some powerful nation must have intrigued with them, and turned their peaceful disposition towards us into hostilities. Great Britain alone has intercourse with those Northern tribes; I therefore infer, that if British gold has not been employed, their baubles and trinkets, and the promise of support and a place of refuge if necessary, have had their effect.

If I am right in this conjecture, war is not to commence by sea or land, it is already begun; and some of the richest blood of our country has already been shed. Yes, Mr. Speaker, in one individual has fallen, the honest man, the orator, and the soldier. That he loved his country none can doubt—he died to preserve its honor and its fame—I mean the late commander of the cavalry; you, sir, who have often measured your strength with his in forensic debate, can attest that he in a good degree, was the pride of the Western country, and Kentucky claimed him as a favorite son. For his loss, with those who fell by his side, the whole Western country is ready to march; they only wait for our permission; and sir, war once declared, I pledge myself for my people—they will avenge the death of their brethren.

Another consideration drawn from our past conduct demands the course we have proposed. In the year 1808, Congress declared that this nation had but three alternatives left—war, embargo, or submission; since that time no advanta-

geous change has taken place in our foreign relations; we now have no embargo, we have not declared war. I then say it, with humiliation, produced by the degradation of my country, we have submitted. Mr. Speaker, I derive no pleasure from speaking in this way of my country, but it is true, and, however painful the truth may be, it should be told.

Another reason operates on my mind; we stand pledged to the French nation to continue in force our non-importation law against Britain; without a violation of national faith we cannot repeal it. What effects is the operation of this law producing? It is demoralizing our citizens; men of commercial habits cannot easily change their course of life; those who have lived in affluence and ease cannot consent to beg for bread. No, sir, they will violate this law, they will smuggle; and, sir, in politics, as in private life, if you wish men to remain virtuous, lead them not into temptation.

This restrictive system operates unequally; some parts of the Union enjoy the same advantages which they possessed when no difficulties attended our foreign relations; others suffer extremely. Ask the Northern man, and he will tell you that any state of things is better than the present; inquire of the Western people why their crops are not equal to what they were in former years, they will answer that industry has no stimulus left, since their surplus products have no markets. Notwithstanding these objections to the present restrictive system, we are bound to retain it—this, and our plighted faith to the French Government, have tied the gordian knot; we cannot untie it; we can cut it with the sword.

This war, if carried on successfully, will have its advantages. We shall drive the British from our Continent—they will no longer have an opportunity of intriguing with our Indian neighbors, and setting on the ruthless savage to tomahawk our women and children. That nation will lose her Canadian trade, and, by having no resting place in this country, her means of annoying us will be diminished. The idea I am now about to advance is at war, I know, with sentiments of the gentleman from Virginia: I am willing to receive the Canadians as adopted brethren; it will have beneficial political effects; it will preserve the equilibrium of the Government. When Louisiana shall be fully peopled, the Northern States will lose their power; they will be at the discretion of others; they can be depressed at pleasure, and then this Union might be endangered—I therefore feel anxious not only to add the Floridas to the South, but the Canadas to the North of this empire.

JOHN RANDOLPH'S ATTACK ON THE COMMITTEE'S REPORT

John Randolph spoke in a piping voice but his brilliance, his caustic wit, and his quick temper were feared by his opponents in the Twelfth Congress. A member of the House since the Sixth Congress, he was an inflexible State Rights Republican who since early in Jefferson's administration had been critical of party measures. In desultory speeches, often studded with irony and abuse, he persistently assailed and ridiculed those who urged war with Britain.

AN insinuation had fallen from the gentleman from Tennessee, (Mr. Grundy.) that the late massacre of our brethren on the Wabash had been instigated by the British Government. Has the President given any such information? Has the gentleman received any such, even informally, from any officer of this Government? Is it so believed by the Administration? He had cause to think the contrary to be the fact; that such was not their opinion. This insinuation was of the grossest kind—a presumption the most rash, the most unjustifiable. Show but good ground for it, he would give up the question at the threshold—he was ready to march to Canada. It was indeed well calculated to excite the feelings of the Western people particularly, who were not quite so tenderly attached to our red brethren as some modern philosophers; but it was destitute of any foundation, beyond mere surmise and suspicion. What would be thought, if, without any proof whatsoever, a member should rise in his place and tell us, that the massacre in Savannah, a massacre perpetrated by civilized savages, with French commissions in their pockets, was excited by the French Government? There was an easy and natural solution of the late transaction on the Wabash, in the well known character of the aboriginal savage of North America, without resorting to any such mere conjectural estimate. He was sorry to say that for this signal calamity and disgrace the House was, in part, at least, answerable. Session after session, their table had been piled up with Indian treaties, for which the appropriations had been voted as a matter of course, without examination. Advantage had been taken of the spirit of the Indians, broken by the war which ended in the Treaty of Greenville. Under the ascendancy then acquired over them,

Annals of Congress, 445-50.

they had been pent up by subsequent treaties into nooks, straightened in their quarters by a blind cupidity, seeking to extinguish their title to immense wilderness, for which, (possessing, as we do already, more land than we can sell or use) we shall not have occasion, for half a century to come. It was our own thirst for territory, our own want of moderation, that had driven these sons of nature to desperation, of which we felt the effects. . . .

He could but smile at the liberality of the gentleman [Felix Grundy], in giving Canada to New York, in order to strengthen the Northern balance of power, while at the same time he forwarned her that the Western scale must preponderate. Mr. R. said he could almost fancy that he saw the Capitol in motion towards the falls of Ohio—after a short sojourn taking its flight to the Mississippi, and finally alighting on Darien; which, when the gentleman's dreams are realized, will be a most eligible seat of Government for the new Republic (or Empire) of the two Americas! But it seemed that "in 1808 we talked and acted foolishly," and to give some color of consistency to that folly, we must now commit a greater. Really he could not conceive of a weaker reason offered in support of a present measure, than the justification of a former folly. He hoped we should act a wiser part—take warning by our follies, since we had become sensible of them, and resolve to talk and act foolishly no more. It was indeed high time to give over such preposterous language and proceedings.

This war of conquest, a war for the acquisition of territory and subjects, is to be a new commentary on the doctrine that Republics are destitute of ambition —that they are addicted to peace, wedded to the happiness and safety of the great body of their people. But it seems this is to be a holiday campaign—there is to be no expense of blood, or treasure, on our part—Canada is to conquer herself—she is to be subdued by the principles of fraternity. The people of that country are first to be seduced from their allegiance, and converted into traitors, as preparatory to the making them good citizens. Although he must acknowledge that some of our flaming patriots were thus manufactured, he did not think the process would hold good with a whole community. It was a dangerous experiment. We were to succeed in the French mode by the system of fraternization—all is French! but how dreadfully it might be retorted on the Southern and Western slave-holding States. He detested this subordination of treason. No—if he must have them, let them fall by the valor of our arms, by fair, legitimate conquest; not become the victims of treacherous seduction.

He was not surprised at the war spirit which was manifesting itself in gentlemen from the South. In the year 1805–6, in a struggle for the carrying trade of belligerent colonial produce, this country had been most unwisely brought into collision with the great Powers of Europe. By a series of most impolitic and ruinous measures, utterly incomprehensible to every rational, sober-minded man, the Southern planters, by their own votes, had succeeded in knocking down the price of cotton to seven cents, and of tobacco (a few choice crops excepted) to nothing—and in raising the price of blankets, (of which a few would not be amiss in a Canadian campaign,) coarse woollens, and every article of first necessity, three or four hundred per cent. And now that, by our own acts, we have brought ourselves into this unprecedented condition, we must get out of it in any way, but by an acknowledgement of our own want of wisdom and forecast. But is war the true remedy? Who will profit by it? Speculators—a few lucky merchants, who draw prizes in the lottery—commissaries and contractors. Who must suffer by it? The people. It is their blood, their taxes, that must flow to support it.

But gentlemen avowed that they would not go to war for the carrying trade—that is, for any other but the direct export and import trade—that which carries our native products abroad, and brings back the return cargo; and yet they stickle for our commercial rights, and will go to war for them! He wished to know, in point of principle, what difference gentlemen could point out between the abandonment of this or of that maritime right. Do gentlemen assume the lofty port and tone of chivalrous redressors of maritime wrongs, and declare their readiness to surrender every other maritime right, provided they may remain unmolested in the exercise of the humble privilege of carrying their own produce abroad, and bringing back a return cargo? Do you make this declaration to the enemy at the outset? Do you state the minimum with which you will be contented, and put it in her power to close with your proposals at her option; give her the basis of a treaty ruinous and disgraceful beyond example and expression? and this too after having turned up your noses in disdain at the treaties of Mr. Jay and Mr. Monroe! Will you say to England, "end the war when you please, give us the direct trade in our own produce, we are content"? But what will the merchants of Salem, and Boston, and New York, and Philadelphia, and Baltimore, the men of Marblehead and Cape Cod, say to this? Will they join in a war professing to have for its object what they would consider (and justly too) as the sacrifice of their maritime rights, yet affecting to be a war for the protection of commerce?

He was gratified to find gentlemen acknowledging the demoralizing and destructive consequences of the non-importation law—confessing the truth of all that its opponents foretold when it was enacted. And will you plunge yourselves in war, because you have passed a foolish and ruinous law, and are ashamed to repeal it? "But our good friend the French Emperor stands in the way of its repeal," and as we cannot go too far in making sacrifices to him, who has given such demonstration of his love for the Americans, we must, in point of fact, become parties to his war. "Who can be so cruel as to refuse him this favor?" His imagination shrunk from the miseries of such a connexion. He called upon the House to reflect whether they were not about to abandon all reclamation for the unparalleled outrages, "insults and injuries" of the French Government, to give up our claim for plundered millions; and asked what reparation or atonement they could expect to obtain in hours of future dalliance, after they should have made a tender of their person to this great deflowerer of the virginity of republics. We had by our own wise (he would not say *wise-acre*) measures, so increased the trade and wealth of Montreal and Quebec, that at last we began to cast a wistful eye at Canada. Having done so much towards its improvement by the exercise of "our restrictive energies," we began to think the laborer worthy of his hire, and to put in claim for our portion. Suppose it ours, are we any nearer to our point? As his Minister said to the King of Epirus, "may we not as well take our bottle of wine before as after this exploit?" Go! march to Canada! leave the broad bosom of the Chesapeake and her hundred tributary rivers—the whole line of seacoast from Machias to St. Mary's, unprotected! You have taken Quebec—have you conquered England? Will you seek for the deep foundations of her power in the frozen deserts of Labrador?

"Her march is on the mountain wave,
  Her home is on the deep!"

Will you call upon her to leave your ports and harbors untouched, only just till you can return from Canada, to defend them? The coast is to be left defenceless, whilst men of the interior are revelling in conquest and spoil. But grant for a moment, for mere argument's sake, that in Canada you touched the sinews of her strength, instead of removing a clog upon her resources—an encumbrance, but one, which, from a spirit of honor, she will vigorously defend. In what situation would you then place some of the best men of the nation? As Chatham and Burke, and the whole band of her patriots, prayed for her defeat in 1776, so must some of the truest friends to their country deprecate the success of our arms against the only Power that holds in check the archenemy of mankind. . . .

Our people will not submit to be taxed for this war of conquest and dominion. The Government of the United States was not calculated to wage offensive foreign war—it was instituted for the common defence and general welfare; and whosoever should embark it in a war of offence, would put it to a test which it was by no means calculated to endure. Make it out that Great Britain had instigated the Indians on the late occasion, and he was ready for battle; but not for dominion. He was unwilling, however, under present circumstances, to take Canada, at the risk of the Constitution— to embark in a common cause with France and be dragged at the wheels of the car of some Burr or Bonaparte. For a gentleman from Tennessee or Gennessee, or Lake Champlain, there may be some prospect of advantage. Their hemp would bear a great price by the exclusion of foreign supply. In that too the great importers were deeply interested. The upper country on the Hudson and the Lakes would be enriched by the supplies for the troops, which they alone could furnish. They would have the exclusive market: to say nothing of the increased preponderance from the acquisition of Canada and that section of the Union, which the Southern and Western States had already felt so severely in the apportionment bill.

THE WAR REPUBLICANS REPLY TO RANDOLPH, ARGUING THE NECESSITY OF WAR

(1) Robert Wright

Wright, a Revolutionary War veteran who had held various offices in his home state of Maryland and had served earlier both in the House and the Senate, was an old Republican. He gave ardent support to the war party.

M<small>R.</small> S<small>PEAKER</small>, I must beg the indulgence of the House while I deliver my opinion on the subject now under consideration, the most important that has been submitted to the Congress of the United States. I, sir, shall take the liberty of varying the question from the honorable member from Virginia (Mr. Randolph,) who yesterday considered it a question of peace or war. I shall consider it as a question of war or submission, dire alternatives, of which, however, I trust no honest American can hesitate in choosing, when the question is correctly stated and distinctly understood. The gentleman from Virginia contends that it is a dispute about the carrying trade, brought on us by the cupidity of the American merchants, in which the farmer and planter have little interest; that he will not consent to tax his constituents to carry on a war for it; that the enemy is invulnerable on the "mountain wave," the element of our wrongs, but should they violate the "natale solum," he would point all the energies of the nation and avenge the wrong. Was that gentleman stricken on the nose by a man so tall that he could not reach his nose, I strongly incline to think his manly pride would not permit him to decline the conflict. Sir, the honorable member is incorrect in his premises, and, of course, in his conclusions. I will endeavor to convince him of this, and shall be gratified if I can enlist his talents on the side of a bleeding country. Sir, the violations of the commercial rights of which we complain do not only embrace the carrying trade, properly so called, but also the carrying of the products of our own soil, the fruits of our own industry; these, although injurious only to our property, are just causes of war. But, sir, the impressment of our native seamen is a stroke at the vitals of liberty itself, and although it does not touch the "natale solum," yet it enslaves the "nativos filios"—the native sons of America; and, in the ratio that liberty is preferable to property, ought to enlist the patriotic feelings of that honorable member, and make his bosom burn with that holy fire that inspired the patriots of the Revolution.

Sir, the carrying trade—by which I mean the carrying articles the growth, produce, or manufacture of a foreign clime—except articles contraband of war —is as much the right of the American people as the carrying the products of their own soil, and is not only secured by the law of nations, but by the positive provisions of the British Treaty. To us, sir, it is an all-important right. We import from the West Indies, annually, property to the amount of forty millions of dollars, for which we pay in the products of our own soil; of this, ten millions only are consumed in the United States, and the surplus thirty millions are exported to foreign countries, on which the American merchant pays three per cent on the duties to the United States, obtains the profits on the freight of thirty millions of dollars, and furnishes a market for American productions to the same amount. . . .

Mr. Speaker, I hope if the gentleman from Virginia will not defend the carrying of foreign articles, he will defend the carrying the products of our own soil, a right most disgracefully violated. When our own citizens have been carrying provisions—the produce of their own soil, in their own ships—to feed the armies of England, and her allies on the continent of Europe, they have been captured on their homeward-bound passage, on their own coast, and condemned in a British Court of Admiralty. If this does not inspire him, yet I am not without hopes that when he reflects on the impressment of our native American seamen, while carrying the products of our own industry to market, thousands of whom, at this moment, are languishing under the ignominious scourge, on board the infernal floating castles of Great Britain, he will feel like an American, devoted to avenge their wrongs. He has said, that if Great Britain had an agency in exciting the Indians to the massacre of the troops under Governor Harrison, he would avenge it. Sir, can he then feel less bound to avenge the slavery and death of American impressed seamen, committed directly by Britons themselves, than the death of citizens by the savages through a British agency? I should like to hear him exercise his logical talent in the discrimination of these cases, which, however profound, would, I presume, be ineffectual to that purpose. Sir, the impressment of American seamen is of ancient date. The outrage was remonstrated against by our WASHINGTON, and by every Administration since, and every diplomatic energy, in every Administration exerted to put a stop to this infamous practice, in vain.

Mr. Speaker, I ask honorable gentlemen if we are not bound by the most solemn ties to protect our seamen by all the lawful means we possess? I have ever considered that protection and allegiance were reciprocal obligations—the counterparts of each other; that the protection of the citizen in his liberty was secured to him by the Constitution, and every member of the Government bound by oath to support that Constitution, securing to him that right. I ask, should an impressed American seaman who had been for seven years under the lash, and whom we had, during that time neglected, be indicted for high treason when found, with our enemies, in arms against us— should he plead specially that fact, would it avail him? And if it would not, how can we neglect to protect him in his liberty, secured by the social compact which we are bound by oath to execute? Mr. Speaker, it is well known that my sympathies have always been enlisted

for this hardy and valuable class of our fellow-citizens, who, though poor, yet as "honest tars," proverbially, in a peculiar manner are entitled to our protection. . . .

But to divert our attention from the wrongs of which we complain, the gentleman from Virginia tells us that our own restrictive system has undone us; that our cotton is reduced to seven cents, and our tobacco to nothing. Sir, there are now no restrictions to the exportation of these articles, and if that had been the cause, on its removal the effect would have ceased with it. No, sir, we are to look for the cause of the reduction of the prices of our cotton and tobacco in the political and commercial history of Europe. The price of cotton depends on the demand for the manufactures of that article; the English-made cottons depended on the continental markets, from which the British manufactures are excluded. The price of tobacco never was materially varied by the consumption in England, but depended on the foreign demand from Great Britain, which, by their exclusion from the continent, is almost entirely arrested. Sir, if we examine, with candor, the cause of the reduction of the prices of these articles, we shall find that the retaliatory system of the two great belligerents produced it: "The British proclamation blockading system," of 1806, induced the continental blockade of 1807, and ultimately the interdiction of all articles the growth, produce, or manufacture of Great Britain to the Continent. . . .

Mr. Speaker, I regret that the gentleman from Virginia should ascribe to gentlemen of the West, a disposition for war, with a view to raise the price of their hemp; or to the gentlemen of the North, with a view to raise the price of their beef and flour. These, sir, are selfish motives, and such I cannot, for a moment, believe, will be taken into consideration; they will, with every other section of the Union, unite in deciding it on its merits; they will count the wrongs we have sus- tained; they will reflect that the honor, the interest, and the very independence, of the United States, is directly attacked; ...

(2) John C. Calhoun

Although Calhoun was only twenty-nine years old in 1811 and was serving his first term in the House, he was made a member of the important Committee on Foreign Relations. He had been elected as a War Republican from South Carolina.

SIR, said Mr. C., the gentleman from Virginia attributes preparation for war to everything but its true cause. He endeavored to find it in the probable rise of the price of hemp. He represents the people of the Western States as willing to plunge our country into war for such base and precarious motives. I will not reason on this point. I see the cause of their ardor, not in such base motives, but in their known patriotism and disinterestedness. No less mercenary is the reason which he attributes to the Southern States. He says, that the non-importation act has reduced cotton to nothing, which has produced a feverish impatience. Sir, I acknowledge the cotton of our farms is worth but little; but not for the cause assigned by the gentleman from Virginia. The people of that section do not reason as he does; they do not attribute it to the efforts of their Government to maintain the peace and independence of their country; they see in the low price of the produce, the hand of foreign injustice; they know well, without the market to the Continent, the deep and steady current of supply will glut that of Great Britain; they are not prepared for the colonial state to which again that Power is endeavoring to reduce us. The manly spirit of that section of our country will not submit to be regulated by any foreign Power. The love of France and the hatred of England has also been assigned as the cause of the present measure. France has not done us justice, says the gentleman from Virginia, and how can we without partiality resist the aggressions of England? I know, sir, we have still cause of complaint against France; but it is of a different character from those against England. She professes now to respect our rights, and there cannot be a reasonable doubt but that the most objectionable parts of her decrees, as far as they respect us, are repealed. We have already formally acknowledged this to be a fact. I, however, protest against the whole of the principles on which this doctrine is founded. It is a novel doctrine, and nowhere to be found out of this House, that you cannot select your antagonist without being guilty of partiality. Sir, when two invade your rights you may resist both or either, at your pleasure. It is regulated by prudence and not by right. The stale imputation of partiality to France is better calculated for the columns of a newspaper than for the walls of this House. I ask, in this particular, of the gentleman from Virginia, but for the same measure which he claims for himself. That gentleman is at a loss

Annals of Congress, 482–3 and 487.

to account for, what he calls, our hatred to England. He asks, how can we hate the country of Locke, of Newton, Hampden, and Chatham; a country having the same language and customs with ourselves, and descending from a common ancestry. Sir, the laws of human affections are uniform. If we have so much to attach us to that country, powerful indeed must be the cause which has overpowered it.

Yes, sir, there is a cause strong enough. Not that occult courtly affection which he has supposed to be entertained for France; but it is to be found in continued and unprovoked insult and injury. A cause so manifest that the gentleman from Virginia had to exert much ingenuity to overlook it. But, sir, here I think the gentleman, in his eager admiration of that country, has not been sufficiently guarded in his argument. Has he reflected on the cause of that admiration? Has he examined the reasons of our high regard for her Chatham? It is his ardent patriotism; the heroic courage of his mind that could not brook the least insult or injury offered to his country, but thought that her interest and honor ought to be vindicated at every hazard and expense.

. . .

Although Mr. Speaker, I believe, under existing circumstances, a war attitude necessary, or at least preparatory steps calculated to meet that event; and although situated as we are, I am for the whole of our legitimate rights; yet sir, I would not be willing to involve the country in war, in defence of the extensive and circuitous carrying trade, separate from the other causes; that is, that we should become carriers for the whole world; as Government receives no benefit from this circuitous carrying trade, only as it is calculated to aggrandize a few individuals engaged in it. I should be for holding fast the claim to the circuitous carrying trade, and would be willing to operate on our enemies by adopting countervailing restrictive systems. But, sir, I would not be willing, that the good of the States, the good of the people, the agriculturists and mechanics, should be put at hazard to gratify the avarice and cupidity of a small class of men, who in fact may be called citizens of the world, attached to no particular country; any country is their country where they can make the most money. But, sir, for what is an inherent right, for what I deem the legitimate, or necessary carrying trade, the liberty of carrying our productions to foreign markets, and with the return cargo, in which agriculture is particularly interested, I would fight in defence of.

(3) William R. King

Most of the War Hawks were relatively young men. King, a War Republican from North Carolina, was serving his first term in the Twelfth Congress. He was twenty-four years old when the session began.

SIR, we have borne with injury, until, in the language of your committee, forbearance has ceased to be a virtue. We have remonstrated, we have appealed to the justice, to the interest, of the two great contending Powers of Europe; every effort proved abortive; our calls for justice were drowned in the declaration that their measures were merely retaliatory, and not intended to interfere with neutral rights; thus, sir, the matter rested, when specific propositions were submitted to each. Yes, sir, by an act which has placed the impartiality of our country beyond the reach of suspicion, we demanded of each the revocation of her obnoxious edicts, as the only means of preserving our friendship. We all know what has been the consequence: France has met our advances, has embraced our propositions. Great Britain not only refuses a repeal on her part, but, while she affects to lament the effects produced on neutral rights, takes the most effectual methods to render them perpetual. Sir, blindness and ignorance itself can no longer be deceived by British policy.

We have been told, sir, that this will be a war for the support of the carrying trade; let me here remark, and I wish to be distinctly understood, as avowing my determination never to give a vote, so long as I have the honor of a seat on this floor, which will involve this country in a war, for the recovery or support of this extraneous species of commerce. I believe I shall not be incorrect when I assert, that nine-tenths of this country never did and never will derive the smallest benefit from it. But, sir, the right to carry in our own ships the produce of our own country to any quarter, not thereby violating the laws of nations, or contravening legitimate municipal regulations, is one which I never will yield; for, sir, in doing so, we paralyze the industry of our citizens; we give a fatal blow to the best interests of our country. Yes, sir, we yield the principle, we invite to further encroachments. Our country, sir, is agricultural, but so intimately blended with commerce, that the one cannot long exist unaided by the other. Sir, I will not yield an inch of ground,

when by so doing, I destroy an essential right of my country—or sap the foundation of that independence cemented by the blood of our fathers. . . . We are told, Mr. Speaker, that we stand pledged to France, that we must become a party with her in this war. Sir, I call upon the gentleman from Virginia to make the assertion good, to fix the imputation upon the Executive or upon this House. Sir, my pledge is to my country, to this very land; here, and here alone, the warm affections of my heart find a point around which to rally. To all other Governments, I am perfectly indifferent—I am no Frenchman, I am no Englishman.

We have been told, sir, that this will be a war of aggrandizement, a war of conquest. I am as little disposed to extend the territory as any other individual of this House. I know that dissimilar interests must and will prevail from a too great extension of our dominion. But, sir, we will not here enter into a discussion, whether an accession of country would or would not conduce to the interests of the Government. Sir, this will be a war forced upon us; we cannot, under existing circumstances, avoid it. To wound our enemy in the most vulnerable part should only be considered. Sir, I trust, if our differences with Great Britain are not speedily adjusted, (of which, indeed, I have no expectation,) we shall take Canada. Yes, sir, by force; by valor; not by seduction, as the gentleman from Virginia expresses it. I have no reliance on their friendship—I hope it will not be calculated on. Sir, I am not deterred from the firm purposes of my mind, by the predictions of the gentleman from Virginia. I have no fears, sir, that the people of our country will desert their Government while asserting the rights of the country; and I must believe, that gentleman's assertion to the contrary notwithstanding, that Virginia will not be the last to afford supplies. We are told, sir, that Republicans are inconsistent; that, in 1798, they refused to raise an army, although General WASHINGTON would be at their head, and that we then had sufficient cause to go to war with the Directory of France. For myself, sir, I was at that period conning the lessons of childhood. I will not now undertake to say, whether, at that time, there was or was not cause for war, as has been de-

clared. To me it matters not. Sir, I am just commencing my political career; I am consistent; I find my country degraded by insults unrevenged; almost ruined by her efforts to preserve friendship with nations who feel power and forget right; and, although I am opposed to the principle of having large standing armies in our country, yet, sir, under these circumstances, I feel justifiable in departing from the general principle. . . .

THE OPPOSITION ARGUMENT

(1) Richard Stanford

Stanford, an "old" Republican from North Carolina, was serving his eighth consecutive term in the House. He was probably the only follower of Randolph left in the House and as such strongly opposed the war.

SIR, we are told war is to be declared in certain events, and that the army proposed is to invade and take the Canadas. We are then to pass out of the limits of the United States and wage a war of the foreign offensive kind! If such was the contemplated use of this army when raised, he was still the more opposed to the measure. He was against the war itself, and the policy of it, and could by no means yield his vote to bring it about. That there was sufficient cause of war, he was ready to acknowledge, and he was not disposed in any the least degree, to palliate the offences of Great Britain, or that of any of the other belligerents, committed on the persons and property of our citizens. All of them had deserved war at our hands, but we had at no time since the commencement of our present Government seen it our interest or policy to give into it, in the open and declared

form, nor that of any other form, except that of a *quasi* character which happened under Mr. Adams's administration. The question never had been whether we had or had not cause of war, but whether the true interest of the United States did not, under all circumstances, call aloud upon us to cherish peace, and to avoid war and its evils as the last of the alternatives before us; and this, said Mr. S., he would be able to show was the Republican doctrine, as well in the old minority times as since that minority grew into a majority. . . .

But, said Mr. S., the gentleman from South Carolina (Mr. CALHOUN) tells us it is a principle of honor in a nation, as in an individual, to resist a first insult. If such doctrine is to be admitted, when should we have had a moment's peace? From one or the other belligerents of Europe, since their late wars commenced,

we have never been without just complaints against them for some violation
of our neutral rights, and of course must
have taken an early share in their wars.
The truth is, we cannot liken, nor will
the similitude hold good between an individual's honor, or his sensibility to it,
and that of a nation's. A single impressment or capture may be well admitted
to form a ground of reprisal and war; but
we should have been a ruined country
long ere now, if, under the existing circumstances of the world, and belligerent
Europe, we had yielded to this quickness
of sensibility, and had gone to war for a
first and single instance of aggression
from either of the belligerents. . . .

. . . Mr. S. said, he could not perceive
how the present, of all others, had become the necessary and accepted time
for war with Great Britain. The attack
on the Chesapeake frigate had been
lately atoned for, to the satisfaction of
our Government; and, he trusted, had
not been so done as to aggravate the crisis of affairs between the two countries.
If calculated to do so, our Government
could not have received it. The impressment of our seamen was a just complaint
against the British Government; but it
commenced under the Administration of
General WASHINGTON, and no one
would say he was less sensible to national
honor and independence than ourselves.
Under all the circumstances of that cause
of complaint, he did not think it a cause
sufficient for him to depart from the neutral ground he had assumed; nor was the
annoyance of our commerce less vexa-
tious in his time than since. In like man-

ner, under Mr. Adams's Administration,
the same complaints existed, though in
that of the latter, not, perhaps, to the
same degree; and, under the eight years
of Mr. Jefferson's Administration, the
same state of things continued, certainly
with increased degree of violence, to
which was also added the more aggravating insult upon the Chesapeake. Mr. Jefferson had never been suspected of partiality for Great Britain, and then, indeed, the accepted time had come for a
war with that Government; all parties
were united, and pledged themselves to
support him in the war. The pulse of the
nation beat high for it. But he felt, because he knew, that peace was the best
interest of his country, and forebore to
call Congress together. He had always
admired the man; but, upon that occasion, he felt more than a sentiment of admiration toward him. When, at length,
wrongs had thus accumulated, and
called for some system of counteraction
and resistance, till negotiation could be
farther tried, the embargo was resorted
to in preference to war; and, when that
was done away, a system of non-intercourse was substituted, and to that again
succeeded the present alternative law of
the same kind; the nonimportation system which has grown out of this with
Great Britain has not been tried one
whole year yet. If gentlemen will have it
that this is the accepted time for war,
how has it happened that we have not
had it before? Our Councils may be presumed to have been as sensible to aggression, and as patriotic to redress it, as
we now are.

(2) *John Randolph*

Randolph's second speech opposing war was one of the longest delivered in the Twelfth Congress. The following contains the gist of his argument.

Bᴜᴛ we are told, and by men of honor too, that we stand pledged to France. I was not surprised, sir, to see this asserted by factious journalists, but I confess my astonishment; nay, my grief and indignation, when I hear it asserted on this floor, by men whom I honor, whom I love, whom I revere! Bound to France, as Sinbad the sailor was bound to the putrifying corpse of his deceased wife. If so, then have we sealed our perdition. Will any man contend that we have the right to transfer to a foreign Despot the power of making war for us, upon whom and when he shall please? No, sir, I deny it; such is not our miserable, our hopeless condition. We are not bound to France, and, so help me God, with my consent, we never shall be so bound. What will your constituents say to this? Suppose they crowd your table with memorials and instructions against this measure, will you reply to them with the coolness of a modern duellist—"We are bound in honor; we are sorry for it, but cannot help it. The sacred trust which you reposed in us we have betrayed; the high attributes of sovereignty, the power of war and peace with which you clothed us for your own good, we have made over, by legislative legerdemain, to the great oppressor of our name and race. We are spell bound, under incantation, and must obey." Will the people endure this? Is the power of making war transferred from the American Congress to France? and by chicanery too?

Bound to France! By what? By a contrivance, an artifice the most bungling—by a quibble which a Newgate solicitor would blush to plead in bar of an indictment for felony. But, sir, if you have sold yourselves into foreign bondage, I pray you to show me the equivalent, the *quid pro quo.* What have you got in exchange from the tyrant of the earth? Where is the mess of pottage, the miserable dish of French broth, of soup maigre, for which you have bartered away your birthright; the birthright of a whole people; the right of self-government; the power over war and peace! Shall we look into the official, responsible correspondence, of our own Government for this equivalent? We have their unquestionable testimony that France has played us false. . . .

. . . our Minister at Paris had been compelled to state to the French Government, "that no appeal to our solemn treaty with the ruler of France, or to the laws of nations," which are the principles of eternal justice and truth, "would be literally to appeal to the dead." And yet, with all this glaring testimony of French perfidy, injustice, injury, and insult, we hear of *pledges to France,* of designating our enemy, and that enemy *not* France. Sir, if you go to war it will not be for the protection of, or defence of your maritime rights. Gentlemen from the North have been taken up to some high mountain and shown all the kingdoms of the earth; and Canada seems tempting in their sight. That rich vein of Gennesee land, which is said to be even better on the other side of the lake than on this. Agrarian cupidity, not maritime right, urges the war. Ever since the report of the Committee on Foreign Relations came into the House, we have heard but one word—like the whip-poor-will, but one eternal monotonous tone—Canada! Canada! Canada! Not a syllable about Halifax, which unquestionably should be our great object in a war for maritime security. It is to acquire a prepondering northern influence, that you are to launch into war. For purposes of maritime safety, the barren rocks of Bermuda were worth more to us than all the deserts through which Hearne and McKenzie had pushed their adventurous researches. Since this great bomb, the report of the Committee, had burst upon the House, Mr. R. had been anxiously waiting for some great political or military projector to point out a way by which we could get at Halifax, or even at Quebec. He had seen and heard nothing that indicated a tolerably correct information of the subject. Whilst England maintained the mastery of the seas, and could throw supplies into them at pleasure, he supposed they were to be starved out. He was forcibly reminded of a ludicrous caricature, published soon after the siege of Gibraltar. That fortress was represented to lie in the moon—and whilst the Duke de Crillon was making passes at it with a small sword, Don Quixote, on his Rosinante, with Sancho (the best and most honest Governor of whom he had ever heard) mounted on Dapple, at his back, exclaimed, with true Castilian gravity to his trusty squire, "we'll starve them out Sancho!" This *tit-bit* Canada, which had inflamed the cupidity of northern contractors, made us forget the disturbances among our savage neighbors—the hostilities committed or meditated along our whole northwestern and southern frontier. Symptoms of discontent were manifesting themselves among the Creeks—in the State of Georgia. As to Louisiana, he did not consider it as an integral part of the United States. We had bought it and might sell it—he felt himself as much at liberty to sell it as to dispose of his own slaves. If we were to have war, he hoped it would be for something of greater national benefit than to enrich the commissaries and contractors from Michillimackinac to Niagara and Frontignac.

(3) Daniel Sheffey

Sheffey was a Federalist from Staunton in the Shenandoah Valley. This area of Virginia had long been a Federalist stronghold.

I HAVE no difficulty in believing, that ever since the year 1806, not only Great Britain, but France also, have given us repeated causes of war, which, according to the former usages of nations, is justified whenever an indignity is offered, or a national right violated. I am not one of those, therefore, who suppose that "Great Britain has done us no essential injury." Far from it. I am fully sensible of the indignities offered to us, and the repeated violations of our rights as a neutral nation on her part; but this is not enough for me. I must be persuaded that there is a rational hope that war will remedy the evil which we experience,

Annals of Congress, 621–26 and 634–35.

and that it will not bring with it others much more to be dreaded than that under which we labor. Were these things as little questionable as the course of the British Government has been unjust, I should have no hesitation in uniting my efforts to obtain justice by force. . . .

On the subject of the impressment of our seamen, much has been said in the course of this debate. The distresses of fifty thousand American citizens on board the British ships of war have been described in feeling language, and painted in glowing colors, particularly by an honorable member from Kentucky, (Mr. JOHNSON.) Without believing that the actual number approaches that supposed, I feel for our unfortunate countrymen in that situation, and readily admit that there is cause of complaint against Great Britain, arising from that source. But, on this subject, it is important to view the question on both sides, to enable us to ascertain whether we are not claiming more than we can ever rationally expect to obtain. Our native citizens, or those who were members of this community at the close of the Revolutionary war, are unquestionably entitled to exemption from impressment. But we claim it for every person who shall sail under our flag—at least, for those that have been naturalized since the period mentioned. I confess I am not disposed to enter into a war for the security on the high seas of the latter class. I think we do enough (more than any other Government on earth does) when we place those persons upon a perfect equality, as it respects the enjoyment of every right within our territorial jurisdiction. So far, no other nation has cause to complain, because we do not interfere with any right claimed by them, either sanctioned by public law, or of a questionable character. But further we cannot go, without

interfering with the claims of other sovereign Powers, sanctioned by long practice and acquiescence. Allegiance is due from every person in a social state to some Government. In the dark ages of superstition and despotism, it was claimed as due by divine right; but since the dawn of civil liberty, it has been considered as a duty growing out of an implied compact between the governors and governed, and indissoluble like other compacts, without the mutual assent of the contracting parties. On this principle is founded the doctrine of perpetual allegiance recognised throughout Europe, and the British pretensions, by which they reclaim their subjects found on board of our merchant vessels, where they allege they are not entitled to protection, no more than enemy's property and contraband goods, for which they have an unquestionable right to search. Thus, while they claim the right of impressing their own subjects only, the similarity of manners and language, and the abuses of power by British officers, causes the impressment of many of our native citizens.

In considering this part of the subject, I deem it unnecessary to investigate the *justice* of the doctrine for which Great Britain contends, or how far it corresponds with the abstract "right of man"; I speak of the fact. It is enough for us to know that these pretensions exist, have long existed, and will not be abandoned. We must be conscious that we cannot *impose our principles* on other nations, with whom it is our interest to cultivate a good understanding; but that on every subject where our rights or pretensions may conflict, both parties must cherish a spirit of conciliation and concession, as the only mode by which we can be brought together to prevent collision, from which neither can derive any substantial benefit. The question is not what we want, but what, under all circumstances, it is possible we can get. I have, therefore, long since thought that our Government ought to abandon the high pretensions of affording security to every person (even aliens) who should sail under our flag, and propose some arrangement to Great Britain, which, while it gave protection to our own native citizen, would prevent our merchants from employing any other during the present war. If these stipulations were reciprocal, every substantial object would be answered. Should Great Britain refuse an overture so manifestly just, it would afford additional cause of complaint, and then we might indulge in the bitter invectives which have been uttered against her.

From what I have said it will be apparent that I do not oppose this measure on the ground that there is not ample cause of war against Great Britain. The reverse is explicitly admitted. But shall the blood and treasure of this nation be lavished against the Orders in Council, as so much paper, or are we to contend for some substantial good, which we should otherwise enjoy, and of which their operation deprives us? I presume there is scarcely a man in this country, however infected he may be with the war mania, who could act so madly, as to propose a warfare to procure the mere nominal repeal of Orders in Council, when it was evident it would be unattended with a single practical benefit. No! the nominal repeal of the Orders in Council is not your object. It is the substantial commercial benefit which you conceive will follow that act, that forms the essence of the controversy. The unmolested commerce to France and her dependencies is the boon for which you are going to war. This is the real object,

disguise it as you will. And it is not the commerce which we formerly enjoyed (as gentlemen would seem to suppose) which is in controversy. Your export commerce to France now consists of our own products only, as appears by the letter of the French Minister on your table. I say our own products, because I suppose the privilege which has been graciously extended to us, of exporting other articles in certain cases under French licenses, will scarcely be insisted on as being anything else but an indignity. The municipal regulations which have been substituted for the Berlin decree, so far as it respects the practical effect, have destroyed by far the most profitable and important branch of our trade to the French Empire, which consisted in the products and manufactures of other countries. Our merchants were in the habit of exporting to the West Indies our flour, beef, pork, livestock, lumber, &c., for which they received in return the products of those islands. The surplus beyond the consumption of this country was exported to the continent of Europe, for which we received in return French wines, brandies, silks, German linens, and bills on London. Of so much more importance was this export trade to us than that of our own commerce, that in 1807, before the British Orders in Council existed, the domestic exports to France (including Belgium) amounted to about two millions seven hundred thousand dollars only; while the amount of exports to the same country of foreign manufactures and products (chiefly colonial) was nearly ten millions. In the same year the whole of our domestic exports to every part of the world, amounted to about forty-eight millions and a half; of which the amount I have stated was exported to France, and about twenty-eight millions to Great

Britain and her possessions and dependencies, in the four quarters of the globe. Since that time she has acquired the French West Indies, the Isles of France and Bourbon in the Indian ocean, the Cape of Good Hope, the Dutch possessions in Asia and America. To these countries in 1807, while under their former dependence, the exports of domestic products from the United States amounted to upwards of four millions of dollars; so that estimating our exports to Great Britain and her present possessions and dependencies as they stood in 1807, the amount would be about thirty-two millions—about two-thirds of the whole amount of our domestic exports to every part of the world. Thus, while we are about engaging in a war for commerce, we abandon the greater, absolutely, and *contend* for the lesser. We relinquish our commerce with Great Britain and her possessions at the threshold, (for during hostilities I presume we shall have none) and go to war for what we can get of the commerce of France, Italy, Holland, Hamburg, and the Hanse Towns. I leave Spain and Portugal and their American provinces out of the question, as the fate of those countries hangs in suspense.

But this is not all. We may expect to see, and the day is not distant, when the dominions of France shall not afford us a market for a single article, but all commerce with her shall either be interdicted by her own Government, or abandoned by our merchants as unworthy their pursuit. Ever since the date of the Berlin decree, and the prostration of the Prussian monarchy, those who gave themselves the trouble to think, and could think, saw that a great and radical change in the state of Europe was intended by the Imperial conqueror, who wields the destinies of the Continent. Whatever the ultimate object might be, it was early perceivable that that mutual dependence which exists between commercial States, so far as it respected the French Empire, was about to be dissolved, and that it was to be dependent no longer upon foreign nations for any supplies. To this, every regulation (ex-territorial or municipal) adopted by its Government has kept a steady eye. They are now staring you full in the face. You see your trade in the colonial products, formerly the most profitable branch of our foreign commerce, totally annihilated. The consumption of tobacco, a great staple of the Middle States, reduced to one-fifteenth of the whole quantity consumed in France, and that monopolized by the French Government, who pays your merchants what its rapacity dictates. You see your cotton, once the great and profitable staple of the South, subjected to such enormous impost duties, as almost amount to a prohibition, for the avowed purpose of encouraging the culture of that article in Italy, and the south of France; your flour and provisions find no market there, because she has a surplus of her own production. The other articles in which we are permitted to trade are so inconsiderable in value that they form no serious item in the account. Besides all this, you see your merchants, after having submitted to the injustice of French regulations, and the rapacity of French officers, compelled to invest the little remnants of the proceeds of their cargoes in French silks, wines, and brandies, in *regulated* proportions. Sir, this detail ought to convince us that a commerce thus shackled and limited is not worthy of the crusade which is meditated, and that the prospect as to its future value is still more gloomy. I believe were the Orders in Council repealed tomorrow, our commerce to France would not be worth two millions, and circumscribed as it already is, as long as the anti-commercial system continues, we may expect that it will daily diminish.

But we have been told that all calculations, as to objects, means, or consequences, are to be laid out of the question, as sordid and low-minded. That, feeling our country's rights violated and her honor assailed, we ought to march heedlessly on to seek redress at every hazard. I confess I was astonished to hear such a course recommended. In the most unimportant concerns of life, a prudent man calls to his aid his best reason and deliberate judgment. But it seems in the great concerns of the nation, where its peace is at stake and its future destiny hazarded, we must close our eyes, set all prudence at defiance, and move boldly on to our object, and not disgrace ourselves by consulting lessons of wisdom and experience which lie in our way. Sir, this nation's honor is the prosperity and happiness of the people. I cannot consent to purchase national misery, even should it be accompanied with what gentlemen call national honor. The abstract notions of honor which regulate the conduct of individuals, and which are valuable in private life, ought not to be a rule of action for wise men to whom are committed the affairs of nations—otherwise we might wage perpetual war. In the whole history of our Government, prudence has been considered as essential to regulating our measures, particularly those which affect foreign nations. We have not suffered ourselves to be led away by our feelings, but were governed by the very calculations which gentlemen now affect so much to despise. . . . Can the waste of our blood and treasure heal the wounds which the nation's fancied honor may have received? Are we to draw upon us all the miseries that attend war, and all the dangers with which it is surrounded,

without any practical good in prospect, when perhaps at the end of seven years we shall be compelled to sit down and acquiesce under the system against which the war is waged, merely to have it to say—that we acted like men of spirit? . . .

The present state of the European world, is the primary cause from which those principles that have so seriously affected our commerce have received their origin. And to me it appears vain to expect that our neutral rights will be respected, until the causes which have subverted every venerable principle, once a rule of conduct between nations, shall no longer exist. We may make arrangements with France for the revocation of her decrees, and with England, for the revocation of her Orders in Council. But there will be no permanent security; we must participate in the evils (in some shape) which have fallen on the community of civilized man. . . .

There is one consideration distinct from all others, which ought to inspire us with caution in entering into the contest between the two great belligerents: England is contending not only for her own existence, but in doing so, she secures us from the attempt to subjugate us to the power of France, to which we should be otherwise exposed. I feel myself under no obligation for any good intention towards us on her part; it is a sense of her own danger, and her struggle for security that produces the effect; but the fact is unquestionably so. Viewing the character of him who has enslaved Europe, I cannot believe otherwise than that if England shall fall, we shall not remain unassailed. . . .

We have been emphatically asked, (by Mr. SPEAKER,) "what are we to gain by peace?" I was astonished at the question. What are we to gain by peace? What are we not to lose by war? Liberty!

security! and happiness! are the great blessings which we hazard! Leave me these, and take your trade to the Continent, or your Orders in Council. With all the difficulties which we encounter, and the ills which befall us, we are still the freest and happiest nation on which the sun shines. I fear, sir, we shall draw upon us the just displeasure of Heaven, if we estimate her bounties, lavished upon us with such a profuse hand, so lightly.

THE REBUTTAL OF THE WAR REPUBLICANS
(1) David R. Williams

Williams had also served in the Ninth and Tenth Congresses. He was chairman of The Committee on Military Affairs and, like the other seven representatives from South Carolina, was a War Republican.

SIR, trade was destroyed by British agency, and it is altogether immaterial whether the destruction was effected by her blockade of France, or by this or that Order of Council; the injury is received, the destruction is effected, the principle is the same. Sir, the injury is not confined to the reduction of the trade to France only, but affects that to Great Britain also, so far as its profits are necessary to maintain that trade. But what is the condition of the commerce with Great Britain now, which he estimates at 32,000,000? Truly miserable. The great staples of your country, wheat and flour excepted, (observe they are not articles of permanent export to Great Britain,) had better be thrown off the wharf than shipped there. Let me suppose the gentleman to be engaged in a particular branch of commerce; that his sales are restricted to a market glutted with from three to ten times the amount of its consumption, would not his ruin be inevitable? How is tobacco affected? Export 75,000 hogsheads to any place where only 15,000 are consumed, and the effect is obvious. Inquire into the state of the cotton market; where is the crop of 1810? A curse to him who meddled with it! Where is that of 1811? Rotting at home in the hands of the grower, waiting the repeal of the Orders in Council. Sir, I know, I feel these to be some of the effects of those orders; yet they must not be resisted, it would be to barter a trade of thirty-two for two! They are mere paper and ink!

But we are going to war for honor; that it seems is a mere bubble. It was astonishing to hear that gentleman, who himself cherishes as high notions of honor as other men, should seek to destroy it in his own country. That which is sacred in an individual, cannot be less so in a nation. Is that proud virtue, that exalted attribute, without which there is neither value nor patriotism in the individual, to be treated with disrespect, to be utterly discarded, when the great concerns of the nation are under consideration? Of what is the nation composed? Of brutes, sir, or men; high-minded, honorable men? He presumed he could offer no outrage so great to that gentleman as the slightest imputation on his honor, and shall that which graces the character of a gentleman be scouted from this House? Shall we, who hold our honor dearer than life and all its blessings, consider that of the nation as a bubble?

Annals of Congress, 686–87.

(2) Henry Clay

*Although Clay had served previously in the Senate, he first took a
seat in the House when elected to the Twelfth Congress. A Republican
from Kentucky, he was made Speaker and assumed the leading role in
promoting entrance into war against Britain.*

WHAT are we to gain by war, has been emphatically asked? In reply, he would ask, what are we not to lose by peace?—commerce, character, a nation's best treasure, honor! If pecuniary considerations alone are to govern, there is sufficient motive for the war. Our revenue is reduced, by the operation of the belligerent edicts, to about six million of dollars, according to the Secretary of the Treasury's report. The year preceding the embargo, it was sixteen. Take away the Orders in Council, it will again mount up to sixteen millions. By continuing, therefore, in peace, if the mongrel state in which we are deserve that denomination, we lose annually, in revenue only, ten millions of dollars. Gentlemen will say, repeal the law of nonimportation. He contended that, if the United States were capable of that perfidy, the revenue would not be restored to its former state, the Orders in Council continuing. Without an export trade, which those orders prevent, inevitable ruin would ensue, if we imported as freely as we did prior to the embargo. A nation that carries on an import trade without an export trade to support it, must, in the end, be as certainly bankrupt, as the individual would be, who incurred an annual expenditure, without an income.

He had no disposition to swell, or dwell upon the catalogue of injuries from England. He could not, however, overlook the impressment of our seamen; an aggression upon which he never reflected without feelings of indignation, which would not allow him appropriate language to describe its enormity. Not content with seizing upon all our property, which falls within her rapacious grasp, the personal rights of our countrymen—rights which forever ought to be sacred, are trampled upon and violated. The Orders in Council were pretended to have been reluctantly adopted as a measure of retaliation. The French decrees, their alleged basis, are revoked. England resorts to the expedient of denying the fact of the revocation, and Sir William Scott, in the celebrated case of the Fox and others, suspends judgment that proof may be adduced of it. And, at the moment when the British Ministry through that judge, is thus affecting to controvert that fact, and to place the release of our property upon its establishment, instructions are prepared for Mr. Foster to meet at Washington the very revocation which they were contesting. And how does he meet it? By fulfilling the engagement solemnly made to rescind the orders? No, sir, but by demanding that we shall secure the introduction into the Continent of British manufactures. England is said to be fighting for the world, and shall we, it is asked, attempt to weaken her exertions? If, indeed, the aim of the French Emperor be universal dominion (and he was willing to allow it to the argument,) what a no-

Annals of Congress, 599–602.

ble cause is presented to British valor. But, how is her philanthropic purpose to be achieved? By scrupulous observance of the rights of others; by respecting that code of public law, which she professes to vindicate, and by abstaining from self-aggrandizement. Then would she command the sympathies of the world. What are we required to do by those who would engage our feelings and wishes in her behalf? To bear the actual cuffs of her arrogance, that we may escape a chimerical French subjugation! We are invited, conjured to drink the potion of British poison actually presented to our lips, that we may avoid the imperial dose prepared by perturbed imaginations. We are called upon to submit to debasement, dishonor, and disgrace—to bow the neck to royal insolence, as a course of preparation for manly resistance to Gallic invasion! What nation, what individual was ever taught, in the schools of ignominious submission, the patriotic lessons of freedom and independence? Let those who contend for this humiliating doctrine, read its refutation in the history of the very man against whose insatiable thirst of dominion we are warned. The experience of desolated Spain, for the last fifteen years, is worth volumes. Did she find her repose and safety in subserviency to the will of that man? Had she boldly stood forth and repelled the first attempt to dictate to her Councils, her Monarch would not now be a miserable captive at Marseilles. Let us come home to our own history. It was not by submission that our fathers achieved our independence. The patriotic wisdom that placed you, Mr. Chairman, said Mr. C., under that canopy, penetrated the designs of a corrupt Ministry, and nobly fronted encroachment on its first appearance. It saw beyond the petty taxes, with which it commenced, a long train of op-

pressive measures terminating in the total annihilation of liberty; and, contemptible as they were, did not hesitate to resist them. Take the experience of the last four or five years, and which, he was sorry to say, exhibited in appearance, at least, a different kind of spirit. He did not wish to view the past further than to guide us for the future. We were but yesterday contending for the indirect trade —the right to export to Europe the coffee and sugar of the West Indies. To-day we are asserting our claim to the direct trade —the right to export our cotton, tobacco, and other domestic produce to market. Yield this point, and to-morrow intercourse between New Orleans and New York—between the planters on James river and Richmond, will be interdicted. For, sir, the career of encroachment is never arrested by submission. It will advance while there remains a single privilege on which it can operate. Gentlemen say that this Government is unfit for any war, but a war of invasion. What, is it not equivalent to invasion, if the mouths of our harbors and outlets are blocked up, and we are denied egress from our own waters? Or, when the burglar is at our door, shall we bravely sally forth and repel his felonious entrance, or meanly skulk within the cells of the castle?

He contended that the real cause of British aggression, was not to distress an enemy but to destroy a rival. A comparative view of our commerce with England and the continent, would satisfy any one of the truth of this remark. Prior to the embargo, the balance of trade between this country and England, was between eleven and fifteen millions of dollars in favor of England. Our consumption of her manufactures was annually increasing, and had risen to nearly $50,000,000. We exported to her what she most wanted, provisions and raw materials for her manufactures, and received in return what she was most desirous to sell. Our exports to France, Holland, Spain, and Italy, taking an average of the years 1802, 3, and 4, amounted to about $12,000,000 of domestic, and about $18,000,000 of foreign produce. Our imports from the same countries amounted to about $25,000,000. The foreign produce exported consisted chiefly of luxuries from the West Indies. It is apparent that this trade, the balance of which was in favor, not of France, but of the United States, was not of very vital consequence to the enemy of England. Would she, therefore, for the sole purpose of depriving her adversary of this commerce, relinquish her valuable trade with this country, exhibiting the essential balance

in her favor—nay, more; hazard the peace of the country? No, sir, you must look for an explanation of her conduct in the jealousies of a rival. She sickens at your prosperity, and beholds in your growth—your sails spread on every ocean, and your numerous seamen—the foundations of a Power which, at no very distant day, is to make her tremble for naval superiority. He had omitted before to notice the loss of our seamen, if we continued in our present situation. What would become of the one hundred thousand, (for he understood there was about that number) in the American service? Would they not leave us and seek employment abroad, perhaps in the very country that injures us?

President Madison's War Message, June 1, 1812

WITHOUT going back beyond the renewal in 1803 of the war in which Great Britain is engaged, and omitting unrepaired wrongs of inferior magnitude, the conduct of her Government presents a series of acts hostile to the United States as an independent and neutral nation.

British cruisers have been in the continued practice of violating the American flag on the great highway of nations, and of seizing and carrying off persons sailing under it, not in the exercise of a belligerent right founded on the law of nations against an enemy, but of a municipal prerogative over British subjects. British jurisdiction is thus extended to neutral vessels in a situation where no laws can operate but the law of nations and the

laws of the country to which the vessels belong, and a self-redress is assumed which, if British subjects were wrongfully detained and alone concerned, is that substitution of force for a resort to the responsible sovereign which falls within the definition of war. Could the seizure of British subjects in such cases be regarded as within the exercise of a belligerent right, the acknowledged laws of war, which forbid an article of captured property to be adjudged without a regular investigation before a competent tribunal, would imperiously demand the fairest trial where the sacred rights of persons were at issue. In place of such a trial these rights are subjected to the will of every petty commander.

The practice, hence, is so far from af-

James D. Richardson, *Messages and Papers of the Presidents 1789–1907* (Washington, D.C.: Bureau of National Literature and Art, 1908), I, 499–505.

fecting British subjects alone that, under the pretext of searching for these, thousands of American citizens, under the safeguard of public law and of their national flag, have been torn from their country and from everything dear to them; have been dragged on board ships of war of a foreign nation and exposed, under the severities of their discipline, to be exiled to the most distant and deadly climes, to risk their lives in the battles of their oppressors, and to be the melancholy instruments of taking away those of their own brethren.

Against this crying enormity, which Great Britain would be so prompt to avenge if committed against herself, the United States have in vain exhausted remonstrances and expostulations, and that no proof might be wanting of their conciliatory dispositions, and no pretext left for a continuance of the practice, the British Government was formally assured of the readiness of the United States to enter into arrangements such as could not be rejected if the recovery of British subjects were the real and the sole object. The communication passed without effect.

British cruisers have been in the practice also of violating the rights and the peace of our coasts. They hover over and harass our entering and departing commerce. To the most insulting pretensions they have added the most lawless proceedings in our very harbors, and have wantonly spilt American blood within the sanctuary of our territorial jurisdiction. The principles and rules enforced by that nation, when a neutral nation, against armed vessels of belligerents hovering near her coasts and disturbing her commerce are well known. When called on, nevertheless, by the United States to punish the greater offenses committed by her own vessels, her Government has be-

stowed on their commanders additional marks of honor and confidence.

Under pretended blockades, without the presence of an adequate force and sometimes without the practicability of applying one, our commerce has been plundered in every sea, the great staples of our country have been cut off from their legitimate markets, and a destructive blow aimed at our agricultural and maritime interests. In aggravation of these predatory measures they have been considered as in force from the dates of their notification, a retrospective effect being thus added, as has been done in other important cases, to the unlawfulness of the course pursued. And to render the outrage the more signal these mock blockades have been reiterated and enforced in the face of official communications from the British Government declaring as the true definition of a legal blockade "that particular ports must be actually invested and previous warning given to vessels bound to them not to enter."

Not content with these occasional expedients for laying waste our neutral trade, the cabinet of Britain resorted at length to the sweeping system of blockades, under the name of orders in council, which has been molded and managed as might best suit its political views, its commercial jealousies, or the avidity of British cruisers.

To our remonstrances against the complicated and transcendent injustice of this innovation the first reply was that the orders were reluctantly adopted by Great Britain as a necessary retaliation on decrees of her enemy proclaiming a general blockade of the British Isles at a time when the naval force of that enemy dared not issue from his own ports. She was reminded without effect that her own prior blockades, unsupported by an adequate naval force actually applied and continued, were a bar to this plea; that executed edicts against millions of our property could not be retaliation on edicts confessedly impossible to be executed; that retaliation, to be just, should fall on the party setting the guilty example, not on an innocent party which was not even chargeable with an acquiescence in it.

When deprived of this flimsy veil for a prohibition of our trade with her enemy by the repeal of his prohibition of our trade with Great Britain, her cabinet, instead of a corresponding repeal or a practical discontinuance of its orders, formally avowed a determination to persist in them against the United States until the markets of her enemy should be laid open to British products, thus asserting an obligation on a neutral power to require one belligerent to encourage by its internal regulations the trade of another belligerent, contradicting her own practice toward all nations, in peace as well as in war, and betraying the insincerity of those professions which inculcated a belief that, having resorted to her orders with regret, she was anxious to find an occasion for putting an end to them.

Abandoning still more all respect for the neutral rights of the United States and for its own consistency, the British Government now demands as prerequisites to a repeal of its orders as they relate to the United States that a formality should be observed in the repeal of the French decrees nowise necessary to their termination nor exemplified by British usage, and that the French repeal, besides including that portion of the decrees which operates within a territorial jurisdiction, as well as that which operates on the high seas, against the commerce of the United States should not be a single and special repeal in relation to the United States, but should be extended to whatever other neutral nations unconnected with them may be affected by those decrees. And as an additional insult, they are called on for a formal disavowal of conditions and pretensions advanced by the French Government for which the United States are so far from having made themselves responsible that, in official explanations which have been published to the world, and in a correspondence of the American minister at London with the British minister for foreign affairs such a responsibility was explicitly and emphatically disclaimed.

It has become, indeed, sufficiently certain that the commerce of the United States is to be sacrificed, not as interfering with the belligerent rights of Great Britain; not as supplying the wants of her enemies, which she herself supplies; but as interfering with the monopoly which she covets for her own commerce and navigation. She carries on a war against the lawful commerce of a friend that she may the better carry on a commerce with an enemy—a commerce polluted by the forgeries and perjuries which are for the most part the only passports by which it can succeed.

Anxious to make every experiment short of the last resort of injured nations, the United States have withheld from Great Britain, under successive modifications, the benefits of a free intercourse with their market, the loss of which could not but outweigh the profits accruing from her restrictions of our commerce with other nations. And to entitle these experiments to the more favorable consideration they were so framed as to enable her to place her adversary under the exclusive operation of them. To these appeals her Government has been equally inflexible, as if willing to make sacrifices of every sort rather than yield to the claims of justice or renounce the errors of a false pride. Nay, so far were the attempts carried to overcome the attachment of the British cabinet to its unjust edicts that it received every encouragement within the competency of the executive branch of our Government to expect that a repeal of them would be followed by a war between the United States and France, unless the French edicts should also be repealed. Even this communication, although silencing forever the plea of a disposition in the United States to acquiesce in those edicts originally the sole plea for them, received no attention.

If no other proof existed of a predetermination of the British Government against a repeal of its orders, it might be found in the correspondence of the minister plenipotentiary of the United States at London and the British secretary for foreign affairs in 1810, on the question whether the blockade of May, 1806, was considered as in force or as not in force. It had been ascertained that the French Government, which urged this blockade as the ground of its Berlin decree, was willing in the event of its removal to repeal that decree, which, being followed by alternate repeals of the other offensive edicts, might abolish the whole system on both sides. This inviting opportunity for accomplishing an object so important to the United States, and professed so often to be the desire of both the belligerents, was made known to the British Government. As that Government admits that an actual application of an adequate force is necessary to the existence of a legal blockade, and it was notorious that if such a force had ever been applied its long discontinuance had annulled the blockade in question, there could be no sufficient objection on the part of Great Britain to a formal revocation of it, and no imaginable objection to

a declaration of the fact that the blockade did not exist. The declaration would have been consistent with her avowed principles of blockade, and would have enabled the United States to demand from France the pledged repeal of her decrees, either with success, in which case the way would have been opened for a general repeal of the belligerent edicts, or without success, in which case the United States would have been justified in turning their measures exclusively against France. The British Government would, however, neither rescind the blockade nor declare its nonexistence, nor permit its nonexistence to be inferred and affirmed by the American plenipotentiary. On the contrary, by representing the blockade to be comprehended in the orders in council, the United States were compelled so to regard it in their subsequent proceedings.

There was a period when a favorable change in the policy of the British cabinet was justly considered as established. The minister plenipotentiary of His Britannic Majesty here proposed an adjustment of the differences more immediately endangering the harmony of the two countries. The proposition was accepted with the promptitude and cordiality corresponding with the invariable professions of this Government. A foundation appeared to be laid for a sincere and lasting reconciliation. The prospect, however, quickly vanished. The whole proceeding was disavowed by the British Government without any explanations which could at that time repress the belief that the disavowal proceeded from a spirit of hostility to the commercial rights and prosperity of the United States; and it has since come into proof that at the very moment when the public minister was holding the language of friendship and inspiring confidence in the sincerity of the negotiation with which he was charged a secret agent of his Government was employed in intrigues having for their object a subversion of our Government and a dismemberment of our happy union.

In reviewing the conduct of Great Britain toward the United States our attention is necessarily drawn to the warfare just renewed by the savages on one of our extensive frontiers—a warfare which is known to spare neither age nor sex and to be distinguished by features peculiarly shocking to humanity. It is difficult to account for the activity and combinations which have for some time been developing themselves among tribes in constant intercourse with British traders and garrisons without connecting their hostility with that influence and without recollecting the authenticated examples of such interpositions heretofore furnished by the officers and agents of that Government.

Such is the spectacle of injuries and indignities which have been heaped on our country, and such the crisis which its unexampled forbearance and conciliatory efforts have not been able to avert. It might at least have been expected that an enlightened nation, if less urged by moral obligations or invited by friendly dispositions on the part of the United States, would have found in its true interest alone a sufficient motive to respect their rights and their tranquillity on the high seas; that an enlarged policy would have favored that free and general circulation of commerce in which the British nation is at all times interested, and which in times of war is the best alleviation of its calamities to herself as well as to other belligerents; and more especially that the British cabinet would not, for the sake of a precarious and surreptitious intercourse with hostile markets, have persevered in a course of measures which necessarily put at hazard the invaluable market of a great and growing country, disposed to cultivate the mutual advantages of an active commerce.

Other counsels have prevailed. Our moderation and conciliation have had no other effect than to encourage perseverance and to enlarge pretensions. We behold our seafaring citizens still the daily victims of lawless violence, committed on the great common and highway of nations, even within sight of the country which owes them protection. We behold our vessels, freighted with the products of our soil and industry, or returning with the honest proceeds of them, wrested from their lawful destinations, confiscated by prize courts no longer the organs of public law but the instruments of arbitrary edicts, and their unfortunate crews dispersed and lost, or forced or inveigled in British ports into British fleets, whilst arguments are employed in support of these aggressions which have no foundation but in a principle equally supporting a claim to regulate our external commerce in all cases whatsoever.

We behold, in fine, on the side of Great Britain a state of war against the United States, and on the side of the United States a state of peace toward Great Britain.

Whether the United States shall continue passive under these progressive usurpations and these accumulating wrongs, or, opposing force to force in defense of their national rights, shall commit a just cause into the hands of the Almighty Disposer of Events, avoiding all connections which might entangle it in the contest or views of other powers, and preserving a constant readiness to concur in an honorable reestablishment of peace and friendship, is a solemn question which the Constitution wisely confides to the legislative department of the Government. In recommending it to their early deliberations I am happy in the assurance that the decision will be worthy the enlightened and patriotic councils of a virtuous, a free, and a powerful nation.

Having presented this view of the relations of the United States with Great Britain and of the solemn alternative growing out of them, I proceed to remark that the communications last made to Congress on the subject of our relations with France will have shewn that since the revocation of her decrees, as they violated the neutral rights of the United States, her Government has authorized illegal captures by its privateers and public ships, and that other outrages have been practiced on our vessels and our citizens. It will have been seen also that no indemnity had been provided or satisfactorily pledged for the extensive spoliations committed under the violent and retrospective orders of the French Government against the property of our citizens seized within the jurisdiction of France. I abstain at this time from recommending to the consideration of Congress definitive measures with respect to that nation, in the expectation that the result of unclosed discussions between our minister plenipotentiary at Paris and the French Government will speedily enable Congress to decide with greater advantage on the course due to the rights, the interests, and the honor of our country.

II. THE HISTORIANS RE-EXAMINE THE CAUSES OF THE WAR OF 1812

Julius W. Pratt: EXPANSIONISTS OF 1812

INTRODUCTION

THE purposes of the present study have been: to examine the development in the Northwest of the demand for the conquest and annexation of Canada; to trace the rise in the South and Southwest of the plan to annex the Floridas and possibly Mexico; to discover the relations of these two proposals to each other and to the question of war with Great Britain; to determine the position of the executive branch of the United States government (especially of Madison and his Secretary of State, Monroe) toward the plans for expansion, north and south; and finally, to determine the causes for the failure, all along the line, of the expansionist hopes with which the war began.

The principal conclusions arrived at may be summarized as follows:

① The belief that the United States would one day annex Canada had a continuous existence from the early days of the War of Independence to the War of 1812. From 1783 to about 1810 such annexation was thought of only as a matter for an indefinite future, the nation during those years having neither the strength, nor any sufficient motive, for taking Canada by force. The rise of Tecumseh, backed, as was universally believed, by the British, produced an urgent demand in the Northwest that the British be expelled from Canada. This demand was a factor of primary importance in bringing on the war.

II. The South was almost unanimous in its demand for the Floridas, for agrarian, commercial, and strategic reasons, and in the spring of 1812 appeared to be in a fair way to accomplish its purpose. In the Southwest, at the same time, there was a lively interest in Mexico and a widely prevalent opinion that it was ready to fall into American hands.

III. Even within the Republican party, there was already a distinct sectional rift between North and South, and neither section was anxious to see the other increase its territory and population. But if both could gain at the same time, and in something like equal proportion, such objections would be obviated on both sides. There is good evidence that, before the declaration of war, northern and southern Republicans came to a definite understanding that the acquisition of Canada on the north was to be balanced by the annexation of the Floridas on the south. Thus the war began with a double-barrelled scheme of territorial aggrandizement.

IV. Both Madison and Monroe, especially the latter as Secretary of State, were wholly in sympathy with the proposal for annexing Florida. The invasion of East Florida by General Mathews in March and April, 1812, was effected with the full knowledge of the administration. Special circumstances forced the government to repudiate Mathews, but the territory he had taken from the Spanish was held for over a year, until Congress had

Reprinted with the permission of the publisher from *Expansionists of 1812* by Julius W. Pratt. Copyright 1925 by the Macmillan Company. Pp. 11–14, 38–59 and 120, 150.

twice refused to sanction the occupation. At the same time, Monroe's official correspondence shows that he never really desired or expected the annexation of Canada.

V. It appears that in the all round failure of the expansionist plans, sectional feeling played a larger part than is commonly supposed. The sectional bargain with which the war had begun broke down. Opposition from northern Republicans combined with Federalists forced the abandonment of East Florida. On the other hand, it is evident that in the utter failure of the efforts to take Canada, not only want of skill and preparation, but also a lack of enthusiasm on the part of the administration and of certain southern men in Congress played a part.

VI. Finally, in the expansionist program with which the war opened, we have the first general appearance of the idea which later received the name of "Manifest Destiny." Although enthusiasts like Jefferson had dreamed years before of a nation destined to embrace the continent, the date usually given for the dawn of "Manifest Destiny" is about 1830.[1] Yet both in the Congressional debates of 1812 and in the contemporary press, particularly that of the Southwest, we find the idea repeatedly expressed. "Where is it written in the book of fate," asked the editor of the Nashville *Clarion* (April 28, 1812), "that the American republic shall not stretch her limits from the Capes of the Chesapeake to Nootka sound, from the isthmus of Panama to Hudson bay?"

[This study] makes no effort to give a full account of the causes of the War of 1812, but deals with one set of causes only. The exclusion from all but briefest mention of the maritime grievances against Great Britain is with no wish to

belittle them. Without them, it is safe to say, there would have been no war, just as the writer feels safe in saying that without the peculiar grievances and ambitions of the West there would have been no war. One set of causes was perhaps as essential as the other.

* * *

THE NORTHWEST AND CANADA

The Eleventh Congress, which assembled toward the end of 1809, seemed at first oblivious of the frontier question. December 18, there was laid before the House a Senate resolution expressing approbation of the conduct of the Executive in refusing to hold further communication with Mr. Jackson, the British minister.[2] The resolution was warmly debated till January 3, when it was passed by a party vote.[3] Here was an opportunity to air all the grievances against the British; yet there was no mention of their plotting with the Indians, although among the speakers were Johnson and McKee of Kentucky and Rhea of Tennessee, all of them among the "war hawks" of the next Congress. Johnson presented a list of the official grievances against Great Britain,[4] and Rhea enumerated the British "aggressions,"[5] but neither had anything to say about Indian affairs. Emott, a New York Federalist, could even taunt the western members with being brave because they were out of danger—"the enemy, before it can reach them, must pass over their neighbors, and thus afford them time to prepare for the conflict."[6] The Westerners made no reply; doubtless they thought the taunt beneath their notice. Yet the fact that it could be made would indicate that the danger of Indian attacks inspired by the

---

[1] Adams, E. D., *The Power of Ideals in American History*, chap. iii.

[2] *Annals of Congress*, 11 Cong., I, 747.
[3] *Ibid.*, p. 1151.
[4] *Ibid.*, p. 796.
[5] *Ibid.*, p. 1022.
[6] *Ibid.*, p. 826.

British was not at that moment prominent in Washington thought or conversation.

But this session of Congress was not to
run to an end without striking a new
note of belligerency, and its members
were soon expressing themselves une-
quivocally for the expulsion of Great
Britain from the continent. In January,
1810, Senator Giles of Virginia introduced a bill for putting the navy in war
trim,[7] and on January 23 he supported
it in a speech. He thought "a war purely
defensive alone justifiable, yet he
thought it perfectly correct to carry on
such a war, when undertaken, offen-
sively; and that it was perfectly justifiable to seize a territory, and appropriate
it as a just retribution for the evils of war
unjustly inflicted by a culpable assailant."[8]
Mr. Giles's biographer believes that the
War of 1812, "if Giles had had his way,
would have been the war of 1810."[9]

Giles was followed a month later by
Clay, then serving out an unexpired
term in the Senate, in a speech which
has been often quoted.

"No man in the nation wants peace
more than I," Clay declared; "but I prefer the troubled ocean of war, demanded
by the honor and independence of this
country, with all its calamities and deso-
lation, to the tranquil and putrescent
pool of ignominious peace. If we can ac-
commodate our differences with one of
the belligerents only, I should prefer that
one to be Britain; but if with neither,
and we are forced into a selection of our
enemy, then am I for war with Britain,
because I believe her prior in aggression,
and her injuries and insults to us more
atrocious in character. . . . It is said, however, that no object is attainable by war
with Great Britain. In its fortunes, we

are to estimate not only the benefit to be
derived to ourselves, but the injury to be
done the enemy. The conquest of Canada is in your power. I trust I shall not be
deemed presumptuous when I state that
I verily believe that the militia of Kentucky are alone competent to place Montreal and Upper Canada at your feet. Is
it nothing to the British nation; is it nothing to the pride of her Monarch, to have
the last of the immense North American
possessions held by him in the commencement of his reign wrested from his
dominion? Is it nothing to us to extin-
quish the torch that lights up savage warfare? Is it nothing to acquire the entire
fur trade connected with that country,
and to destroy the temptation and opportunity of violating your revenue and
other laws?"[10]

Johnson, in the House, spoke in April
in similar tone: "Why have not the people complained of the increase of the
army and navy under the last years of
Mr. Jefferson's administration? Because
they believed one should have been sent
to the Canadas, and the other to drive
smuggling vessels from our waters; and
the only complaint made is, that we have
failed to use the physical force of the nation to chastise the aggressions of other
nations." Johnson made plain his desire
"to maintain our rights, maritime and territorial . . . and drive our enemies from
North America."[11]

Johnson spoke of driving the British
from the continent as one of three possible courses to be pursued. He had not
yet touched the joyous note of Manifest
Destiny. That honor was reserved for
Clay. In the final session of the Eleventh
Congress, in the debate on the West
Florida bill, Clay declared: "I am not,
sir, in favor of cherishing the passion of
conquest. But I must be permitted to con-

[7] Ibid., p. 526.
[8] Ibid., p. 539.
[9] Anderson, William Branch Giles, p. 155.

[10] Annals of Congress, 11 Cong., I, 579, 580.
[11] Ibid., II, 1867, 1871.

clude by declaring my hope to see, ere long, the *new* United States (if you will allow me the expression) embracing not only the old thirteen States, but the entire country east of the Mississippi, including East Florida, and some of the territories to the north of us also."[12]

The Eleventh Congress had improved upon its immediate predecessor in boldness of talk if in nothing else, and the change was most noticeable in the Westerners. They had taken, as we have seen, a strong expansionist tone. The conception of war had advanced in two years from defensive to offensive. The change was doubtless due to various causes—perhaps most of all to sheer exasperation at the long continued dilatory fashion of handling the nation's foreign affairs. But in the West there was another circumstance which must have had a very pronounced effect in altering the attitude of the people toward the British in Canada. We have seen that in the years 1807, 1808, and 1809, the people of Kentucky showed little concern over the reports and rumors of the work of British agents among the Indians. But by 1810 the West was becoming aware of a new and really serious Indian menace. "By April, 1810," says Eggleston, "there was a general conviction on the part of the whites that the plans of Tecumseh and the Prophet were really hostile to the United States."[13] Furthermore, it was known or strongly suspected that the British were lending sympathy and support to these Indian leaders, who sought to make their resistance to land sales "a dam in the progress of the great waters of the white advance."[14] A new series of reports from territorial governors and others, in the

summer and fall of 1810, told of British influence at work among the Indians, and the western press reflected similar views.[15]

Throughout the year 1811, alarm at the menace of Tecumseh's confederacy

[15] Harrison wrote from Vincennes, July 4, 1810: "The treaties made by me last fall, were concluded upon principles as liberal toward the Indians as my knowledge of the views and opinions of the government would allow. . . . But, sir, the President may rest assured, that the complaints of injury, with regard to the sale of lands, is a mere pretense, suggested to the prophet by British partisans and emissaries." To Secretary Eustis. Dawson, *Harrison*, p. 151. About this time, too, Governor Harrison learned that "a Miami chief, who has just returned from his annual visit to Malden, after having received the accustomed donation of goods, was thus addressed by Elliot, the British agent: 'My son, keep your eyes fixed on me—my tomahawk is now up—be you ready, but do not strike till I give the signal.'" *Ibid.*, p. 153. The incident may be fictitious, but it doubtless represents what the West was thinking. From Chicago and St. Louis came reports of Indian hostility and approaching war; and from the latter place it was reported that the Sacks had "absolutely acceded to the confederacy [Tecumseh's], and a party of them had gone off to Detroit [Malden presumably is meant], no doubt for arms and ammunition." *Ibid.*, p. 177.

While Harrison was receiving these reports, Captain Johnston was writing from Fort Wayne to the Secretary of War that "about one hundred Sawkeys have returned from the British agent, who supplied them liberally with everything they stood in want of. The party received forty-seven rifles, and a number of fusils, with plenty of powder and lead. This is sending firebrands into the Mississippi country, inasmuch as it will draw numbers of our Indians to the British side, in the hope of being treated with the same liberality." Aug. 7, 1810. *Am. State Papers, Ind. Aff.*, I, 799.

A month later (September 11, 1810) the Kentucky *Gazette* copied from the *Western Sun* an article from the editor of the latter paper, describing the recent interview between Governor Harrison and Tecumseh. "We have always been of opinion," said the writer, "that the confederacy which has been formed by the Prophet, was the effect of British intrigue; and we have never doubted that the secret agents of that power, which are known to exist in every part of America, but particularly in the Indian country, gave it all the confidence in their power."

[12] *Ibid.*, 3 sess., p. 63.
[13] Eggleston, *Tecumseh and the Shawnee Prophet*, p. 162.
[14] Anderson, "The Insurgents of 1811." *A. H. A. Report*, 1911, p. 171.

and conviction that the British were instrumental in its formation and support grew rapidly among government officials and the people of the West. Governor Harrison wrote in February to the Secretary of War: "If the intentions of the British Government are pacific, the Indian department of Upper Canada have not been made acquainted with them: for they have very lately said every thing to the Indians, who visited them, to excite them against us."[16]

In July a group of citizens of Knox County, Indiana, met at Vincennes and adopted resolutions demanding that the Indian settlement at Tippecanoe—one hundred and fifty miles up the Wabash—be broken up. The wish was natural, in view of the serious menace which the Prophet's town held over the heads of the Knox County settlers;[17] but it was significant that the British were charged with responsibility for the whole situation. "We are fully convinced," said the resolutions, "that the formation of the combination, headed by the Shawanee prophet, is a British scheme, and that the agents of that power are constantly exciting the Indians to hostilities against the United States."[18] Similar views were reflected in resolutions adopted by residents of St. Clair County, Illinois, which mentioned "the seditious village of Peoria, the great nursery of hostile Indians and traitorous British Indian traders."[19]

Meanwhile the Kentucky Gazette was warning its readers of the British-Indian menace in outspoken language:

"It would seem from the attitude of the Indians—the combination of the Northern and Southern tribes—the conference at Malden—the circumstances attendant on the mission of Foster—the late arrival of regular troops in Canada, that the British ministry were planning 'another expedition.' . . .

"From the friendly course pursued by Mr. Jefferson, towards our red neighbors, and which has been followed by Mr. Madison, we had supposed the Indians would never more treat us otherwise than as brethren. But we have been mistaken—British intrigue and British gold, it seems, has greater influence with them of late than American justice and benevolence. . . . We have in our possession information which proves beyond doubt, the late disturbances to be owing to the too successful intrigues of British emissaries with the Indians."[20]

Governor Harrison, representative of "American justice and benevolence" toward the Indians, was at this time planning to open the way to a military career by an attack on the Indian village at Tippecanoe.[21] But he knew that war with England was probable, and suspected that the regiment of regular troops now on their way to him from Pittsburgh, were destined "to our frontiers bordering on Upper Canada." More important than his own ideas on the subject was his estimate of the spirit of the western people, whom he knew if any one knew them. "The people of this Territory [Indiana] and Kentucky," he wrote, "are extremely pressing in offers of their service for an expedition into the Indian Country. Any number of men might be obtained for

[16] Am. State Papers, Ind. Aff., I, 800.
[17] Adams, United States, VI, 78, 79.
[18] Am. State Papers, Ind. Aff., I, 802.
[19] Ibid., I, 803.

[20] Kentucky Gazette, Aug. 27, 1811. The same article was printed in the Chillicothe (Ohio) Independent Republican, Sept. 6, 1811. The Circleville Fredonian (successor to the last named paper) printed similar articles Sept. 19 and Oct. 16. The issue of Oct. 16 also contained a report from Nashville that "propositions have been made the Chickasaw Indians by the British, through the Northern Indians, to join in a war against the U. States."
[21] Adams, United States, VI, 84, 85.

this purpose or for a march into Canada."[22]

Early in September it was reported to Harrison "that defection is evidenced amongst all the Tribes from the Wabash to the Mississippi and the Lakes. That the Indians of the Wabash, Illinois, etc., have recently visited the British agent at Malden. That they are now returning from thence with a larger supply of goods than is ever known to have been distributed to them before. That rifles or fusees are given to those who are unarmed and powder and lead to all. And that the language and measures of the Indians indicate nothing but war."[23] Harrison passed on the information to the War Department a few days later (September 17, 1811), with additional details of the extent of British subsidies: "A trader of this country was lately in the King's store at Malden, and was told that the quantity of goods for the Indian department, which has been sent out this year, exceeded that of common years by £ 20,000 sterling. It is impossible to ascribe this profusion to any other motive than that of instigating the Indians to take up the tomahawk; it cannot be to secure their trade, for all the peltries collected on the waters of the Wabash, in one year, if sold in the London market, would not pay the freight of the goods which have been given the Indians."[24]

Harrison, however, went on to say that, "although I am decidedly of opinion that the tendency of the British measures is hostility to us, candor obliges me to inform you, that, from two Indians of different tribes, I have received information that the British agent absolutely dissuaded them from going to war against the United States." That the compulsion of candor was necessary to bring the governor to pass on this last bit of information is an interesting commentary on his state of mind; but the information itself is perfectly consistent with the other facts of the situation. General Brock wrote, after Harrison's battle with the Indians, that the latter had been "implicitly told not to look for assistance from us," but the phrase occurs in a letter whose main purpose was to point out how the effective aid of the Indians was to be secured and used against the Americans.[25] Throughout the period of the rise of Tecumseh, the British had dissuaded the Indians from beginning a war against the United States; but the purpose of this policy was to allow time for the consolidation of the confederacy, that the aid of the Indians might be the more effective when needed.[26]

Early in November came Harrison's badly managed campaign ending in the battle of Tippecanoe.[27] From the facts already presented it is clear that the blood there shed would be added to the grievances already existing against the British and would bring the West to an eagerness for war without precedent in the entire controversy. "The *blood of our murdered countrymen must be revenged,*" wrote Andrew Jackson to Harrison. "I do hope that Government will see that it is necessary to act efficiently and that this hostile band which must be excited to war by the secret agents of Great Britain must be destroyed."[28] The battle of Tippecanoe gave inestimable support to the war party in the Twelfth Congress, now assembled in Washington for its first session.

The war party, composed of western

---

[22] *Burton Hist. Coll. Pamphlets,* No. 6, p. 217.
[23] *Ibid.,* p. 218.
[24] *Am. State Papers, Ind. Aff.,* I, 801.

[25] *Mich. Pioneer & Hist. Coll.,* XV, 57, (Dec. 2, 1811.)
[26] Adams, *United States,* VI, 85.
[27] *Ibid.,* VI, chap. v.
[28] *Burton Hist. Coll. Pamphlets,* No. 6, p. 263.

men and "radical, expansionist, malcontent politicians of the east," which had existed in Congress since 1810 at least,[29] found itself in full control when the Twelfth Congress met. Clay, the most prominent of the "war hawks," came now to the House of Representatives, where he was at once chosen speaker. He was supported in his warlike policy by members from the frontier sections of the northern states, such as Peter B. Porter of New York and John A. Harper of New Hampshire; by almost the entire delegation of the western states—Worthington of Ohio and Pope of Kentucky, both in the Senate, were the only important exceptions—by a fair proportion of the members from Pennsylvania, Virginia, and North Carolina; and by a very able and aggressive group of young men from South Carolina and Georgia—Calhoun, Cheves, Lowndes, Crawford, Troup, and others—men who had reasons of their own for promoting a war of expansion.

It was soon apparent that the war to which this party was committed was to be no such purely defensive war as the Tenth Congress had contemplated, but that it was to be waged aggressively and with the conquest of Canada as a major object. Some Easterners might agree with Monroe that Canada might be invaded, "not as an object of the war but as a means to bring it to a satisfactory conclusion."[30] but the West was more of the mind of a correspondent of the Philadelphia Aurora, "who wrote that if England were to restore all impressed seamen and make compensation for all her depredations we should listen to no terms that did not include Upper Canada."[31]

President Madison's annual message, delivered to Congress on November 5, contained language that could plainly be interpreted as meaning war. After touching upon the obdurate persistence of Great Britain in attacking American commerce, he went on to say: "With this evidence of hostile inflexibility, in trampling on rights which no independent nation can relinquish, Congress will feel the duty of putting the United States into an armor and an attitude demanded by the crisis, and corresponding with the national spirit and expectations."[32] To deal with that part of the message concerned with foreign relations, Speaker Clay appointed a select committee, upon which he placed a group of the most reliable war men—Porter, Calhoun, Grundy, Harper, and Desha.[33] The committee reported on November 29 a set of six resolutions recommending an increase of ten thousand men for the regular army, a levy of fifty thousand volunteers, the outfitting of all vessels of war not in active service, and the arming of merchant vessels.[34]

It was in the House debate on these resolutions that the war party frankly revealed their designs upon Canada. Mr. Porter, chairman of the committee, speaking on December 6, explained that in addition to the injury which American privateers could inflict upon British commerce, "there was another point where we could attack her, and where she would feel our power still more sensibly. We could deprive her of her extensive provinces lying along our borders to the north. These provinces were not only immensely valuable in themselves, but almost indispensable to the existence of Great Britain, cut off as she now in a

[29] Anderson, William Branch Giles, p. 173.
[30] Writings of James Monroe, V, 205.
[31] Anderson, "Insurgents of 1811," A. H. A. Report, 1911, I, 172.

[32] Annals of Congress, 12 Cong., I, 13.
[33] Ibid., I, 342, 343.
[34] Ibid., I, 377.

great measure is from the north of Europe. He had been credibly informed that the exports from Quebec alone amounted during the last year, to near six millions of dollars, and most of these too in articles of the first necessity—in ship timber and in provisions for the support of her fleets and armies. By carrying on such a war as he had described . . . we should be able in a short time to remunerate ourselves tenfold for all the spoliations she had committed on our commerce."[35]

Grundy of Tennessee, three days later, dwelt upon the peculiar advantage to the Westerner to be derived from war. "We shall drive the British from our Continent —they will no longer have an opportunity of intriguing with our Indian neighbors, and setting on the ruthless savage to tomahawk our women and children. That nation will lose her Canadian trade, and, by having no resting place in this country, her means of annoying us will be diminished."[36] Rhea of Tennessee was equally explicit upon the object of the war—"That all that part of North America which joins the United States on the Northeast, North, and Northwest, shall be provided for in a mode which will forever thereafter put it out of the power of Great Britain, or of any British agent, trader, or factor, or company of British traders to supply Indian tribes with arms or ammunition; to instigate and incite Indians to disturb and harass our frontiers, and to murder and scalp helpless women and children."[37]

Two members of the House, one from Kentucky and one from New Hampshire, expounded the doctrine of Manifest Destiny. "I shall never die contented," announced R. M. Johnson, "until I see her

[Great Britain's] expulsion from North America, and her territories incorporated with the United States. . . . In point of territorial limit, the map will improve its importance. The waters of the St. Lawrence and the Mississippi interlock in a number of places, and the great Disposer of Human Events intended those two rivers should belong to the same people."[38] "The northern provinces of Britain are to us great and valuable objects," proclaimed Harper of New Hampshire. "Once secured to this Republic, and the St. Lawrence and the Lakes become the Baltic, and more than the Baltic to America; north of them a population of four millions may easily be supported; and this great outlet of the northern world should be at our command for our convenience and future security. To me, sir, it appears that the Author of Nature has marked our limits in the south, by the Gulf of Mexico; and on the north, by the regions of eternal frost."[39]

While Congress debated, reports continued to come in of British agents at work among the Indians. As a matter of fact, it would appear that presents to the Indians, and particularly ammunition, were less at this time than previously. Claus wrote General Brock from Amherstburg in June, 1812, that during the last six months the Indians had received only 1211 pounds of powder—"nineteen hundred and twenty-one pounds less than at former periods—of lead, not one ounce has been issued to them since last December."[40] But a letter from Fort Wayne in February stated that two British emissaries had recently passed that way on a mission to the Prophet, and that "their business was to invite all the Indians to meet at Malden very early in

[35] *Ibid.*, I, 416.
[36] *Ibid.*, I, 426.
[37] *Ibid.*, I, 640.

[38] *Ibid.*, I, 457, 458.
[39] *Ibid.*, I, 657.
[40] *Mich. Pioneer & Hist. Coll.*, XV, 89.

the spring." Any event of this kind would of course receive the most unfavorable interpretation. The same letter gave other disturbing reports: "The Pottawatamy chief, Marpack, has been in the neighborhood of Malden since August last. . . . He has about one hundred and twenty of the best warriors in this country with him. . . . I know this chief is hostile inclined towards the United States, and have no hesitation in saying, that he is kept at that place by the British agents at Malden."[41]

If their relations with the Indians constituted a standing reason for driving the British from Canada, a special reason was furnished by the publication of the Henry Letters, for Henry had been in the employ of the Governor-General of Canada.[42] "Can any American, after this discovery," wrote Congressman Desha to a friend in Kentucky, "doubt the propriety of ousting the British from the continent, or hesitate in contributing his proportionable part of the expense which will necessarily be incurred in the laudable undertaking?"[43]

The West no longer needed any such promptings from its representatives in Washington. The rise of Tecumseh and the Prophet, the battle of Tippecanoe, the outspoken position of their congressmen, together with the current belief that the British were behind all their Indian troubles, had resulted in an insistent demand from the Westerners for the conquest of Canada. The Lexington *Reporter* published in January a *"Franklinian Prescription—To cure Indian hostilities, and to prevent their recurrence:* Interpose the American arm between the hands of the English and their savage allies. This done, the occupation of the Canadas,

New Brunswick and Nova-Scotia, would give us perpetual concord with the Indians; who would be obliged *to depend upon us* for supplies of Blankets, knives, gun-powder, etc."[44]

The Kentucky Legislature, which in the crisis of 1807–1808 had made no official mention of the border question, in its resolutions of February, 1812, added to Great Britain's violations of American rights at sea her practice of "inciting the savages (as we have strong reasons to believe) to murder the inhabitants of our defenceless frontiers—furnishing them with arms and ammunition lately, to attack our forces; to the loss of a number of our brave men."[45]

Another indication of public opinion in Kentucky is the character of the toasts proposed at a Washington's Birthday dinner in Lexington. The banqueters drank to such toasts as *"Great Britain, when she comes to her senses—*If she continues lunatic, *Canada* and our arms!" or *"The American Congress—*If they barter the nation's honor under the false idea of temporary popularity, may they meet with the just scorn of an indignant people!"[46]

Public opinion in Ohio paralleled closely that of Kentucky. The Circleville *Fredonian* declared the "indignant spirits" of Americans could be appeased only "by the restoration of our rights, or the conquest of Canada."[47] Correspondents of Senator Thomas Worthington believed that if war came, "we would attack [and] conquer Cannady & humble their overbearing pride," or hoped that American troops would "sever Upper Canada from the British without delay."[48]

[41] *Am. State Papers, Ind. Aff.,* I, 805.
[42] Adams, *United States,* VI, chap. ix.
[43] *The Reporter* (Lexington, Ky.), Mar. 24, 1812.

[44] *Ibid.,* Jan. 21, 1812.
[45] *Ibid.,* Feb. 15, 1812.
[46] *Kentucky Gazette,* Feb. 25, 1812.
[47] *Fredonian,* Feb. 12, 1812. See also *ibid.,* Mar. 18, 1812.
[48] James Caldwell to Worthington, Zanesville,

As the year advanced, the tone of the press grew even more determined. The *Fredonian* saw no hope of peace and security from the savages until "another WAYNE shall force *them* to become our friends, and another WASHINGTON exterminates from the Canadas, the base remains of royal perfidy." The British "must be for ever driven from all their possessions in America." The same paper professed itself eager to undertake a war against both France and Great Britain when it appeared that neither nation was willing to recognize American rights.[49] In April the *Kentucky Gazette* stated: "Great Britain has determined not to recede, and Congress seem at last to have got in earnest, and appear disposed to prepare for war. . . . The recruiting service has been actually commenced in various places, and large bodies of militia are to be raised to march for Detroit and other parts of our frontier. This is all preparatory to the invasion of Canada, now more than ever necessary, as presenting whilst in the possession of Britain, a never failing source of Indian hostility. Until those civilized allies of our Savage neighbors, are expelled from our continent, we must expect the frequent recurrence of the late scenes on the Wabash."[50]

The same paper could not suppress its wrath when the *National Intelligencer*, reputed to be the administration organ, hinted that war might yet be avoided. "Notwithstanding a mass of evidence of this kind [i.e. as to captures, impress-

ment, Henry plots, etc.], the Intelligencer may talk of *negociation* and '*honorable accommodation*' with England; but when we view the effects of her policy in the *West*—when we hear of the tragic scenes that are now acting on our frontiers, after the slaughter of Tippecanoe, it is really surprising to hear that there is any doubt about the '*active preparations for warlike operations*' . . . We will only add, at this time, that we should much like to know the price which the 'Intelligencer' would receive as a compromise for the scalps of *Western Farmers*."[51]

On May 26, three weeks before the declaration of war, the *Gazette* gave what appears like a parting injunction to Congress: "Can it be expected that those savage butcheries will have an end until we take possession of Malden and other British forts on the Lakes? And must the settlements in our territories be entirely destroyed, and the blood of the women and children drench the soil before this can be done? . . . What will our Congress say?" In similar tone the *Reporter* of May 30 declared: "Britain has commenced war in the Western Country, equally so as France would have done, was she to burn New York. The citizens of the Eastern States, and members in Congress, may abandon 7,000 seamen—they may term it, a *trifling impropriety* on the part of England, but the old Revolutionary Heroes here are not to be deceived by the misrepresentations of any man whatever. The Government MUST not abandon the Western Country to the British."

Thus by the end of the spring of 1812, the whole frontier country from New Hampshire to Kentucky was insisting that the British must be expelled from Canada. The demand had been of slow

---

Dec. 14, 1811. J. van Horne to Worthington, Zanesville, April 13, 1812. *Worthington, MSS.* For other expressions of the war spirit in Ohio, see Duncan McArthur to Worthington, Feb. 20, 1812; J. M. Couch to Worthington, Mar. 14, 1812; Levi Barber to Worthington, May 17, 1812. *Ibid.*
[49] *Fredonian*, Apr. 8, May 2, May 30, June 13, 1812.
[50] *Kentucky Gazette*, Apr. 14, 1812.

[51] *Ibid.*, Apr. 21, 1812.

growth. Taking its origin from the ideas of Revolutionary statesmen, it was fed from various sources—from jealousy of the British fur trade, from exasperation at British contempt for the American flag at sea, from the alluring vision of a continent destined to recognize a single sovereignty—but unquestionably most of all from the conviction that the British in Canada were in unholy alliance with the western Indians, and that only by cutting off the Indians from British support could the West gain peace and security. Only thus could the Westerner be free to continue that policy of "justice and benevolence" toward the Indians, which consisted in pushing the boundaries of the white settlements ever farther into the Indian country.[52] Other motives—commercial, political, punitive—played a part; but the overmastering desire of the people of the Northwest was to feel free to develop their country without peril from those Indian conspiracies which were universally believed to have their origin in British Canada.

* * *

THE LURE OF THE
SPANISH PROVINCES

If the frontiersman of the Northwest demanded war with Great Britain as in-

dispensable, his kinsman of the southern border at least saw in it a means of fulfilling his expansionist dreams. The past two years had done much to give him what he thought his territorial rights, but much remained to be gained. The Spanish still held Mobile and Pensacola, St. Mark's and St. Augustine, and the American troops that held the country between the St. John's and the St. Mary's rivers were, it was supposed, about to be withdrawn.

The demand for the annexation of all Florida was more insistent than ever. Georgians like Floyd, Mitchell, Troup, and Crawford—the last two influential members of the war party in Congress—held the acquisition of East Florida essential to the prosperity, to the very safety, of their state. The Augusta *Chronicle*, cited on a previous page, hoped for "some new measures for the purpose of placing the whole of that colony under the control of the United States." Out in Mississippi Territory, the news of the occupation of East Florida aroused a lively hope of similar action farther west. "There is no doubt," wrote a recent settler at St. Stephens, to a friend in the East, "but Mobille and Pensacola will share the same fate in a few weeks, which no doubt will occation considerable action in this quarter during this summer, and all the citizens in this part of the country are much gratified at the Idea of the United States getting Possession of this Southern Coast, as it is certainly of all importance to the citizens of this country."[53] The Nashville *Clarion*, quoting at length from the Congressional Report of 1803 on the navigation of the southern rivers, and explaining in detail

---

[52] For further discussions of this phase of the question see Slocum, *The Ohio Country between the Years 1783 and 1815*; Lewis, "A Re-analysis of the Causes of the War of 1812," *Americana (American Historical Magazine)*, VI, 506–516; 577–585; Coleman, "The Ohio Valley in the Preliminaries of the War of 1812," *Miss. Valley Hist. Review*, VII, 39–50. Abel, Annie H., *The History of Events Resulting in Indian Consolidation West of the Mississippi*, A. H. A. *Reports*, 1906, Vol. I, especially chap. iii. L. M. Hacker, "Western Land Hunger and the War of 1812" (*Miss. Valley Hist. Rev.*, X, 365–395), minimizes the Indian menace and suggests land hunger as the motive of the West. I am unable to agree with his conclusions.

[53] James Bradberry to A. D. Murphy, St. Stephens, M. T., Apr. 21, 1812. *Papers of Archibald D. Murphy*, I, 58.

how Tennessee's transportation difficulties would be solved by the opening of the Alabama and Tombigbee, declared that "No part of the union can be so much interested in the acquisition of West Florida as the State of Tennessee. . . . The Floridas will soon be occupied by American troops."[54]

But if the whole southern border was eager to take what remained of Florida, war with England seemed to afford a perfectly clear occasion for doing so. Spain was England's ally in the European war, and it was safe to assume that Spanish harbors in America would be open to British fleets and armies. As a simple measure of self-defense, the occupation of Florida seemed to many indispensable, and it was commonly assumed at the South that war with England meant war with Spain, or at least the forcible occupation of all Florida.

The notion of a war at once against England and Spain had been broached by Jefferson in 1807, in which case, he declared, "our southern defensive force can take the Floridas."[55] Mathews had alluded to a similar connection when he instructed the "discontents" of East Florida "not to expect that prompt and efficient aid from the United States, if our negotiation with the British Minister terminates auspiciously for us, that they might in the other event expect."[56] Expansionists like Clay and Harper, when they hurled defiance at Great Britain, had spoken in one breath of the nation's prospective conquests on the St. Lawrence and the Gulf of Mexico. Grundy of Tennessee, in the war debate in December, 1811, stated that he felt anxious "not

only to add the Floridas to the South, but the Canadas to the North of this empire."[57] and he wrote to Jackson that in case of war "the Canadas & Floridas will be the Theatres of our offensive operations."[58]

Jackson himself, when shortly after the declaration of war he called upon his division of Tennessee militia to be in readiness, assured them that it was in West Florida that their arms should find employment.[59] Jefferson, writing of the mustering of the militia in his Virginia county in June, 1812, said that "the only inquiry they make is whether they are to go to Canada or Florida."[60]

In Georgia it was generally assumed that war with Great Britain would mean the certain seizure of all of Florida that remained unoccupied. "Had we no other claim on Florida or Spain," said the Augusta *Chronicle* in May, "sound policy would dictate the propriety as well as necessity of retaining possession of it till the close of the war we are now on the eve of commencing with an ally of that country."[61] On the day preceding the declaration of war, the Republican citizens of Milledgeville passed resolutions approving the war measures against Great Britain, and declaring their belief that with war in prospect the occupancy of East Florida was "essential to the interests of the country and the safety of our southern frontier."[62] A letter from Milledgeville dated July 8, 1812, reported that Governor Mitchell, who was

---

[54] Copied in Niles' *Register*, III, 52–53, Sept. 26, 1812.
[55] *Writings of Thomas Jefferson*, V, 164.
[56] Above, p. 83.

[57] *Annals of Congress*, 12 Cong., I, 427.
[58] Grundy to Jackson, Dec. 24, 1811. *Jackson Papers*, MSS., Vol. 9.
[59] Bassett, *Andrew Jackson*, I, 79.
[60] Jefferson to Madison, June 6, 1812. *Writings of Thomas Jefferson*, VI, 58.
[61] Above, note 114.
[62] *Republican and Savannah Evening Ledger*, June 25, 1812.

at St. Mary's, had received news of the declaration of war, and, "considering that the Spaniards and British are in alliance both offensive and defensive, and that the vital interests of this state and the honor of the United States are implicated and will be hazarded by suffering the occupancy of East Florida by the banditti now in possession"—not the "patriots" evidently, to whom the term might have been applied, but the Spanish governor and his negro and Indian auxiliaries—"he will be detained until the reinforcements he has sent for and which are now assembling on the Oconee River, are received."[63] Mitchell himself explained later to the Georgia legislature the light in which, prior to the declaration of war, he had viewed the situation. "The confidence with which I anticipated the declaration of war against Great Britain," said the governor, "led me with equal confidence to anticipate an enlargement of the powers of the President, by congress, as the necessary consequence, having for its object the entire occupancy of East and West Florida."[64]

War with Great Britain, then, meant, to the average Southerner, war also with Spain, and the completion of the annexation of the Floridas. To the people of the Southwest it meant the possibility of even greater things. The old dream of revolutionizing Mexico and, if not actually annexing it to the United States, at least profiting by its agricultural, mineral, and commercial wealth, revived with new vigor. The Southwest tried to persuade itself that the Federal government favored such plans, quoting cryptic passages from "prints known to be in the interest of the administration," and citing the promotion of Colonel Pike, an avowed annexationist, and his position then in command of the troops on the border, as evidence that an invasion was contemplated.[65] A writer signing himself "Americus" contributed to the Nashville *Clarion* of April 28 a long article in which "Manifest Destiny" ran riot.

"The Canadas," wrote Americus, freed from the chains of an European master, shall take the rank of an independent state; or, too weak for sovereignty, shall hover under the wings of the American eagle. . . . The Floridas will sink into the confederation of American states. . . . Whilst our eastern and southern brethren are purchasing renown in arms, and extending the limits of the republic, are we condemned to remain inactive . . . ? No, citizens of the West! a destiny still more splendid is reserved for you. Behold the empire of Mexico, a celestial region, whose valiant sons are now struggling for their liberties as we struggled for ours thirty years ago. . . . Here it is that the statesman shall see an accession of Territory sufficient to double the extent of the republic; where the merchant shall see commercial resources unrivalled in other countries; the farmer, a luxuriant soil and delicious climate, where the financier shall be dazzled with gold and silver mines; while the ardent and generous mind, in the idea of establishing a new republic . . . shall deliver himself up to an enthusiasm of glory. . . . Besides, where is it written in the book of fate that the American republic shall not stretch her limits from the capes of the Chesapeake to Nootka sound, from the isthmus of Panama to Hudson bay?"[66]

Thus while the Northwesterner ex-

---

[63] *National Intelligencer*, July 21, 1812.
[64] *Niles' Register*, III, 193, Nov. 28, 1812.

[65] Nashville *Clarion*, Apr. 30, May 5, 1812.
[66] Nashville *Clarion*, Apr. 28, 1812. Editorially the paper commended the article to its readers, and suggestively followed it up with a series of historical and descriptive articles about Mexico.

pected to take Canada as a result of war with Great Britain, southern men generally expected to complete the seizure of Florida from Great Britain's ally, Spain, while the more ambitious expansionists of the Southwest dreamed of further aggressions upon the Spanish territories, which should end in making the United States co-extensive with the continent of North America.

SECTIONAL POLITICS

If we should locate on a map of the United States the homes of those men in Congress who were most outspoken for war and annexation, and plot from these points the line of maximum war and expansionist sentiment, we should find our line to be the circumference of a crescent with one end in New Hampshire and the other in Savannah, Georgia. Beginning with John A. Harper in the former state, we should pass westward through the home of Peter B. Porter, near Buffalo, New York, thence southwestward through the country of Clay and Johnson in Kentucky, Grundy and Campbell in Tennessee, down through the Abbeville section of South Carolina, the home of Calhoun, and finally to Savannah, in the district represented by George M. Troup. From end to end the crescent traversed frontier territory, bordering foreign soil, British or Spanish, or confronting dangerous Indian tribes among whom foreign influence was suspected and feared. And the men who came from these districts to Washington displayed many of the characteristic frontier traits. They had national patriotism, to the point sometimes of chauvinism, resenting with a new bitterness their country's wrongs and scorning the pacific measures hitherto used to repel them. They had unlimited faith in their country's future, believ-

ing its destined limits to be no less than the eastern and western oceans, the Gulf of Mexico and the "regions of eternal frost." Hence they were for a war which should at the same time defend the country's rights and expand its boundaries; they would punish British insults with the sword, wresting Canada from Great Britain and the residue of the Floridas from her weak ally, Spain.

Nothing could better demonstrate the frontier character of the war spirit than to observe its progressive decline as we pass from the rim of the crescent to its center at the national capital. Expansionist enthusiasm declined even more rapidly. Thus Cheves and Lowndes of South Carolina, Charlestonians both, were good war men but felt little interest in expansion even at the south.[67] In New York, the two senators, Smith from Long Island, and German from a mid-state county, though both Republicans, voted frequently with the anti-war party; German eventually voted against the declaration of war. A step nearer to Washington we have, on the south, Stanford of North Carolina and Randolph of Virginia in the House and Giles of Virginia in the Senate; on the north, Samuel Smith of Maryland and Michael Leib of Pennsylvania, both in the Senate—a group of Republicans who perhaps did more than the Federalists to embarrass the government in its war measures. Randolph was on principle opposed to war with Great Britain and had only contempt for talk of annexing Canada. Stanford apparently took his views from Randolph. But the Senate clique composed of Giles, Samuel Smith and Leib formed a faction whose ruling principle, if we may believe Henry

[67] Both opposed the bill for the occupation of East Florida, June, 1812. See below, pp. 100–101. *Annals of Congress*, 12 Cong., Part II, p. 1684.

Adams, was their hatred of Gallatin, and whose course in Congress was shaped more with a view to embarrassing the Treasury than to serving the interests of their country. Leib and his friend, Duane, publisher of the Philadelphia *Aurora*, had quarrelled with Gallatin long before over the patronage; Smith, over the administration of the Navy Department by his brother, Robert Smith. The exact cause of Giles's hatred of Gallatin is not clear, but it was whispered that he resented Madison's failure to make him (Giles) Secretary of State or to send him on an important foreign mission. He was described as "deadly hostile to Mr. Monroe, and not much in *love* with Mr. Madison."[68]

These men, representing points far distant from the frontier, formed the nucleus of the anti-administration faction in the Senate. They were on occasion reinforced by Senators from nearer the border. German of New York had affiliations with the group, and his colleague Smith sometimes voted with them. Gilman of New Hampshire had covertly opposed Madison's election and could not be counted on to support the administration. Governor Plumer had no confidence in his Republicanism.[69] More surprising was the defection of two western senators, Worthington of Ohio and Pope of Kentucky. Worthington, as his diary shows, was little impressed by reports of British intrigues among the Indians; he deplored the horrors of war and saw its approach with grave misgivings. He had, moreover, changed his politics several times, and his allegiance to the Republican

party was thought to be insecure.[70] Pope, singularly enough, had described himself four years before as a straight administration man, standing high both "on the score of talents and Republicanism," and had added that "except Breckenridge no man from the West ever had more popularity in Congress."[71] In 1810–1811 he had joined Henry Clay in leading the fight for the administration's plan to annex West Florida.[72] Then he had violated the instructions of the Kentucky legislature in supporting the recharter of the United States bank, for which he both voted and spoke, and as a result had been read out of the party by his constituents. He now generally worked with the Giles clique.[73] Both Pope and Worthington were out of touch with Republican sentiment in the states they represented.

As there were men from the border who opposed the war, and cared nothing for territorial expansion, so there were men from the older states and districts who warmly supported both. Macon of North Carolina and Matthew Clay of Virginia, and a considerable part of the Pennsylvania delegation showed unquestioned zeal for the war program and the annexation of Canada. In general, however, our thesis holds good—that enthusiasm for war and annexation was at its height at the periphery of the crescent, while faction flourished most luxuriantly near the center.

[68] John A. Harper to William Plumer, Mar. 15, 1812. *William Plumer Letters, MSS.*, 1809-1815, p. 221. Same to same, June 14, 1812. *Ibid.*, p. 330.
[69] Harper to Plumer, Mar. 15, 1812. *Ibid.*, p. 221. Plumer to Harper, Mar. 31, 1812. *Ibid.*, p. 222.

[70] Worthington's *MS. Diary* in Library of Congress. Entries for Dec. 16, 1811, May 27 and June 14, 1812. War once declared, he was resolved to give the administration loyal support. See also Chillicothe *Independent Republican*, Sept. 27, 1810.
[71] Pope to Ninian Edwards, Jan. 9, 1808. *The Edwards Papers: Chicago Hist. Soc. Collections*, III, 33–34.
[72] Anderson, *William Branch Giles*, p. 159.
[73] Kentucky *Gazette*, Mar. 26, 1811, June 9, 1812. *Annals of Congress*, 11 Cong, 3 sess., pp. 219, 346.

It is near the center too that we find all that remained of Federalist strength outside its northeastern stronghold. For whereas, in the Twelfth Congress, New Jersey had no Federalist members and Pennsylvania but one in a delegation of eighteen, Maryland contributed three Federalists, Virginia six, and North Carolina two.[74]

Our analysis thus far has regarded only the contrasting views and factions within the Republican party. It has ignored what was obviously a factor of vast importance, the Federalism of the Northeast. In Massachusetts, New Hampshire, and Vermont, all states with large frontier elements, the Republicans were for the moment in control; the elections of 1812 were to turn them out in both New Hampshire and Massachusetts. Connecticut, Rhode Island, and Delaware were in almost undisputed Federalist control. New York was about to convert a Republican majority of twelve to five (in its delegation to Congress) to a Federalist majority of nineteen to eight, and to elect a Federalist senator.

The Federalist party, grounded chiefly in the mercantile and financial interests of the coast towns, the college-bred professional men, the more solid and "respectable" elements in society, was fairly homogeneous in its creeds of both foreign and domestic politics. Abroad, it looked upon Napoleon as Anti-Christ and endorsed Pickering's famous toast, "The world's last hope—Britain's fast-anchored Isle." In home affairs,

it was convinced, not without cause, by the measures of the last few years, that the Republican administration had deliberately resolved to ruin its commerce and dissipate its prosperity. Holding these views, it could see no worse national crime than a war against England which would render indirect aid to Napoleon, and no worse disaster to its own interests than a form of expansion which would mean new states to increase the Republican strength in Congress. Its attitude toward the pending measures is easy to deduce.[75] The Federalists were in a small minority in the Twelfth Congress in both House and Senate, but their six votes in the Senate, when combined with those of recalcitrant Republicans, were often enough to defeat important administration measures.[76]

Upon the question of war with Great Britain, a miscalculated notion of political expediency led the Federalists in Congress into an equivocal position. Failing to take the correct measure of the rising war spirit, they held to the belief, expressed two years before by Quincy of Massachusetts, that the Republicans "could not be kicked" into hostilities. Quincy regarded the war talk indulged in by the Westerners, when Congress convened, as "ludicrous"; and he wrote to Harrison Gray Otis in Boston, suggesting the proper stand for Federalists to take.

"Instead of suffering themselves to believe and inculcating the belief in others," he wrote, "that the design of administration is a British war; let them understand, and let them make it apparent to the people, that their real design is to embarrass commerce and annihilate its in-

---

[74] Niles' *Register*, I, 233–234. In Virginia, the Federalist stronghold was not, as we might expect, in the tide-water region, but west of the Blue Ridge, in the Valley of Virginia, and still farther to the west on the Great Kanawha. Ambler, *Sectionalism in Virginia*, pp. 87–93. For a brief account of Federalism in North Carolina at this time, see Dodd, *Life of Nathaniel Macon*, pp. 242, 275.

[75] Morison, *Harrison Gray Otis*, II, chap. xix.
[76] The actual strength in the Twelfth Congress was: Senate, Rep. 28, Fed. 6; House, Rep. 105, Fed. 37. Niles' *Register*, I, 233–234.

fluence, as a part of a system, which has for its objects, the present advancement of their personal views and the permanent elevation of the interests of the planting States over the commercial. Let them go further. Let them set themselves about convincing the people of our section of the country that the present situation of the commercial part of the country *is worse than any war, even a British,* and that if administration mean to force us to take one, or the other, that although they cannot justify the principle of such war, yet that in its political effects, foreign war in any supposable calamity is preferable to the evils we now feel and may fairly anticipate."[77]

Acting upon this principle, Otis and other Federalists voted in favor of the administration's war measures. Two unnamed Federalists even told the British minister that they would help to involve the government in an inevitably unsuccessful war, which must lead in turn to the downfall of the Republicans and an early peace under a Federalist administration. But shrewd as the plan was, it could command little support from the great body of Federalists who regarded England's power as the "bulwark of the liberties of this country and of mankind." In Quincy himself it was based on a firm belief that the war talk was "bluff," and he in the end voted against the declaration of war.[78]

The strength of the Federalists' opposition to a British war was almost equalled by their antipathy to territorial expansion and the admission of new states in the southwest. Such accretions, they felt, could only increase the number of the "planter States" and so intrench in power those interests which wished to destroy New England commerce. Thus, in January and February, 1811, they had opposed in a body the bill authorizing the occupation of the Floridas and the enabling act which permitted the people of Orleans territory to form a constitution and seek admission as a state. Against the second measure Quincy had argued at length, taking the ground that the Constitution contained no warrant for the grant of statehood to a territory not within the original national domain; and his speech contained the famous declaration: "If this bill passes, it is my deliberate opinion that it is virtually a dissolution of this Union; that it will free the States from their moral obligation, and, as it will be the right of all, so it will be the duty of some, definitely to prepare for a separation—amicably if they can, violently if they must."[79]

It is thus apparent that the nation in 1812 was divided by a two-fold cleavage. There was, first, the line between East and West, or more accurately, between the frontier crescent from New Hampshire to Georgia, and the more settled and stable portions of the country. Here war men and annexationists, all Republicans, were opposed, in the north by New England Federalism, and in the Middle States, from New York to North Carolina, by the factious and anti-war Republicans with a scattering of Federalists. Cutting across this line at right angles was a second line of cleavage between the commercial and the planter states, the free and the slave states. In terms of bitterness and distrust, this line

---

[77] Morison, *Harrison Gray Otis,* II, 30–34.
[78] *Ibid.,* II, pp. 34–36. Adams, *United States,* VI, 174, quoting Foster's dispatches to his government.

[79] Vote on the Florida bill, *Annals of Congress,* 11 Cong., 3 sess., pp. 374, 1138. Vote on enabling act for Orleans territory, *ibid.,* pp. 127, 577. Quincy's speech, *ibid.,* pp. 524ff.

cut far deeper than the first. Between East and West there might be disagreement in interests and ideals; between New England Federalism and Southern Planterdom there was implacable enmity. Thus the Federalists formed the nucleus for a sectional Northern party. How real was the tie that bound northern Republicans to their political allies in the South?

Up to the winter of 1812 northern Republicans had as a rule supported southern policies. The enabling act for Orleans territory had been opposed by only three Republicans in the Senate—Gilman of New Hampshire, German of New York, and Reed of Maryland—and one in the House—Van Rensselaer of New York. The bill for the occupation of Florida had received even fuller support, Reed of Maryland casting the only northern Republican vote against it. On these measures, too, the few southern Federalists had voted with their New England colleagues.

But before the Twelfth Congress had been long in session, it appeared that a sectional cleavage existed which might split both parties into northern and southern groups, and that even the Westerners of the extreme war party were susceptible to jealousies between North and South. The measure which brought to light this sectional cleavage was the bill for the new apportionment of representation on the basis of the Third Census. November 22, 1811, the House passed a bill providing that there should be, in the next Congress, one representative for each 37,000 of the population. The Senate changed the unit to 35,000. Senator Cutts of New Hampshire explained the situation in a letter of December 11 to Governor Plumer.

"The settling the ratio upon the cen-

sus," wrote Cutts, "has become a very difficult thing and is exciting a great deal of interest; the House fixed it at 37,000, upon the principle, that was the highest at which no state would lose a member, an unfortunate number for N[ew] H[ampshire], but when the bill came into the Senate other things were taken into view, particularly what bearing it would have upon the Presidential election and it was found that 35,000 would best suit the Northern interest. Accordingly, a rare thing, all the States north of the Potomac united in that. It has now become a party question North ag[ains]t South."[80]

The amended measure was returned to the House and debated December 5. Gholson of Virginia called attention to the disadvantages which the South would suffer under the Senate's figure. Nine northern states, he showed, with a population of three and one-half millions, would have unrepresented fractional populations of 82,000; eight southern states with a population ("federal number") of three millions, would have unrepresented fractional populations of 167,000, which on a *pro rata* basis was 98,000 more than their due proportion. "By adopting the Senate's amendment," Gholson continued, "the Eastern States, moreover, gain nine Representatives, the Southern States two only. The ratio of 35,000 is therefore peculiarly unequal in its operation, and consequently unjust. . . . Geographical comparisons and local distinctions are at all times, sir, repugnant to my feelings. . . . But I have been driven into the remarks which I have made by the course this business and the debate upon it have taken. . . . If I understood the gentleman [Mr. Smilie, a

[80] *William Plumer Letters, MSS.*, 1809–1815, pp. 175–176.

Pennsylvania Republican, whose remarks are not reported], he said that the secret was, that the Southern people wanted the preponderance. . . . Whatever may be intended, the observation is unmerited, and I repel it."[81]

The House refused to agree to the Senate amendment and returned the bill to the upper body. The Senate voted, 18 to 16, to adhere to its amendment, Federalists and northern Republicans from New Hampshire to Maryland uniting to form the majority. With the exception of the senators from New Jersey and Ohio, who voted against the measure, a solid North faced a solid South across the Potomac. The House thereupon yielded, and by a majority of 72 to 62 accepted the Senate amendment. Here again, party lines gave way to sectional. Virginia, the Carolinas, Kentucky, and Tennessee cast solid votes against acceptance, Federalists voting with Republicans. The only affirmative votes from the South were two from Georgia. From north of the Potomac there were fourteen negative votes, one (a Federalist) from Maryland, one from Ohio, and the remainder from Pennsylvania and New Jersey.[82]

Governor Plumer of New Hampshire scented serious danger in the sectional antagonism here displayed. "There is no state of parties, that can ever arise in this country," he wrote to Senator Cutts, "that, in my opinion, is so much to be deprecated, as that designated by *geographical* lines. Such parties are dangerous to the Union—and if they become strong they or the Union of the States must soon be dissolved. . . . But I hope that Congress in settling this question will not by their debates and votes proclaim to the world, that they believe the

interests of the North and of the South are in reality hostile to each other. Your present course is, you may rely upon it, highly grateful to certain federal characters in New England—who have long privately supported a division of the States."[83]

If, as appears from the foregoing, there was developing a sectional consciousness which could on occasion transcend the older partisan lines, allying Federalists and Republicans of either section against the other; if political leaders of each section, regardless of party, distrusted any addition to the power of the other, it would seem natural that northern and southern Republicans should have viewed differently the programs of territorial expansion now before the country. Would not northern Republicans, though till now they had supported the occupation of Florida and the admission of new states in the southwest, fear the additional power that such measures would eventually give the South? And, on the other hand, could a southern Republican like Grundy, who opposed an appropriation for the "New York Mammoth Canal" because, as he wrote Jackson, by such a measure "no other purpose could be answered except to increase the power of the Northern Section of the Union,"[84] favor wholeheartedly the annexa-

[81] *Annals of Congress*, 12 Cong., I, pp. 411–412.
[82] *Ibid.*, pp. 31, 558.

[83] *William Plumer Letters*, MSS., 1809–1815, p. 179. It is interesting to compare these words of Plumer's with some expressions of his earlier Federalist days. "We have no part in Jefferson and no inheritance in Virginia," he had written in 1804. "Shall we return to our homes, sit under our own vines and fig trees and be separate from slave-holders?" And again in the same year: "I fondly hope I shall live to see the righteous separated from the wicked by a geographical line." Bruce, *John Randolph of Roanoke*, I, pp. 176–177.
[84] Grundy to Andrew Jackson, Feb. 12, 1812. *Jackson Papers*, MSS., Vol. 9.

tion of Canada, which would mean eventually the addition of several northern states? Kentuckians, perhaps, might wish with equal zeal for expansion north and south, for Kentucky was at once so southern as to feel a vital interest in the river outlets to the Gulf, and so northern as to be tragically alive to the dangers arising from British manipulation of the Indians of the Northwest. But the states north and northeast of Kentucky could hope to receive no benefit, and must see a political danger, in annexing Florida, while the states to the south and southeast must feel a similarly lukewarm interest in the annexation of Canada.

If, however, the two measures could go hand in hand, and Canada and Florida be at once added to the national domain, then the expansionists of both sections could fulfill their hopes, and the balance of power would remain substantially unchanged. When, therefore, we find southern men advocating the conquest and annexation of Canada, we may suspect that they expected in return northern support for their own annexation program. If they were to carry through their designs upon Florida, they must hold New York, Pennsylvania, and Ohio true to the alliance which the Apportionment Bill had shown to be in danger, and Canada was to be the price. That some such bargain was actually made seems clear from events during this session of Congress, but it came only after months of maneuvering.

Grundy of Tennessee had no desire, as we have seen, to increase the relative power of the northern states. Nevertheless, he was willing to give a *quid pro quo,* and it was by him that the possibility of a mutually advantageous arrangement was first proclaimed in Congress. "The idea I am about to advance," he

declared in the House, December 9, "is at war, I know, with the sentiments of the gentleman from Virginia [Randolph]; I am willing to receive the Canadians as adopted brethren; it will have beneficial political effects; it will preserve the equilibrium of the Government. When Louisiana shall be fully peopled, the Northern States will lose their power; they will be at the discretion of others; they can be depressed at pleasure, and then this Union might be endangered—I therefore feel anxious not only to add the Floridas to the South, but the Canadas to the North of this empire."[85]

The offer of a bargain was sufficiently plain, and it was probably in reply to it that John A. Harper of New Hampshire, one of the most insistent of the northern expansionists, announced three weeks later his belief that "the Author of Nature has marked our limits in the south, by the Gulf of Mexico; and on the north, by the regions of eternal frost."[86]

Grundy and Harper thus seemed to be in entire agreement, and it is possible that the two Republican wings might have come to an early understanding had not John Randolph taken it upon himself to warn his southern colleagues of the fraud about to be perpetrated upon them, and incidentally to drag the sectional issue into full daylight.

"He could but smile," Randolph declared, December 10, "at the liberality of the gentleman [Grundy] in giving Canada to New York, in order to strengthen the Northern balance of power, while at the same time he forewarned her that the Western scale must preponderate. Mr. R[andolph] said he could almost fancy that he saw the Capitol in motion towards the falls of the Ohio—after a

[85] *Annals of Cong.,* 12 Cong., I, 426–427.
[86] *Ibid.,* p. 657.

short sojourn taking its flight to the Mississippi, and finally alighting in Darien; which, when the gentleman's dreams are realized, will be a most eligible seat of government for the new Republic (or Empire) of the two Americas! . . . He was unwilling, however, under present circumstances, to take Canada at the risk of the Constitution—to embark in a common cause with France and be dragged at the heels of the car of some Burr or Bonaparte. For a gentleman from Tennessee or Genesee, or Lake Champlain, there may be some prospect of advantage. Their hemp will bear a great price by the exclusion of foreign supply. In that too the great importers were deeply interested. The upper country on the Hudson and the Lakes would be enriched by the supplies for the troops, which they alone could furnish. They would have the exclusive market; to say nothing of the increased preponderance from the acquisition of Canada and that section of the Union [sic], which the Southern and Western States had already felt so severely in the apportionment bill."

Mr. Randolph then turned to the defenceless state of the Chesapeake and the danger which, with the militia drawn off to Canada, might arise from the negro population, corrupted, so he declared, by the French Revolution.[87]

Six days later Randolph renewed his attack:

"Sir, if you go to war it will not be for the protection of, or defence of your maritime rights. Gentlemen from the north have been taken up into some high mountain and shown all the kingdoms of the earth; and Canada seems tempting in their sight. That rich vein of Genesee

land, which is said to be even better on the other side of the lake than on this. Agrarian cupidity, not maritime right, urges the war. Ever since the report of the Committee on Foreign Relations came into the House, we have heard but one word—like the whippoor-will, but one eternal monotonous tone—Canada! Canada! Canada! Not a syllable about Halifax, which unquestionably should be our great object in a war for maritime security. It is to acquire a preponderating northern influence, that you are to launch into war."[88]

Yet again, on January 9, 1812, Randolph declaimed upon the danger of sectional jealousy inherent in the expansion policy:

"You are laying the foundation for a secession from the Union—on the north, by the possession of Canada, and on the borders of the Ohio, for another division. The Ohio has been made the line between the slave-holding States and those which hold no slaves. He need not call the attention of the House to this distinction, nor to the jealousies and animosities growing out of the subject."[89]

John Randolph's influence was at this time at perhaps its lowest ebb. A great man he had been and was again to be. But at the time when war was being debated in Congress, he had cut himself off from his party and stood almost alone. Scarcely a Republican, save Stanford of North Carolina,[90] came orally to his support. Are his speeches, which have been quoted at seemingly disproportionate length, therefore unimportant? Perhaps the question should be answered in the light of subsequent events. If we reflect how, a few years later, Randolph became

[87] *Ibid.*, pp. 441 ff.

[88] *Ibid.*, p. 533.
[89] *Ibid.*, p. 712.
[90] *Ibid.*, pp. 664 ff.

the organizer of the slave-holding South,[91] we may perhaps see in his frank declaration of sectionalism on the Canadian question the first step in his return to power. If this were true, we should expect to see some suggestions of his influence in the conduct of southern war Republicans. In fact, some such suggestions do appear.

The tactics of Giles, Smith, and Leib in the Senate had forced upon the administration, instead of the additional regular army force of 10,000 for which it had asked, a measure providing for an additional force of 25,000—a force which, because of the long term of service and other unfavorable conditions, no reasonable man expected to see recruited.[92] The alternative was the use of militia, or volunteers, which was authorized to the number of 50,000 men. (Bill approved Feb. 6, 1812.) But no sooner had debate begun upon the Volunteer Bill than the perplexing question arose whether under the Constitution, these volunteers could be used beyond the boundaries of the United States. The question was debated at wearying length and with a variety of opinions.[93] Congress declined to settle it one way or the other, and passed the bill with the matter still in doubt; but the very doubt made it clear that no energetic use could be made of these forces for purposes of invasion. This unfortunate situation affected northern and southern aspirations quite differently. West Florida was already, by law and proclamation, American soil. East Florida, by the Act of January 15, 1811, could almost be so regarded. Technically, therefore—even

had the southern militia had those "constitutional scruples" on the subject from which Jackson declared they were free[94] —they might nevertheless have been marched into Florida, and no very large force, presumably, would be needed for its occupation. But Canada was plainly foreign soil; its invasion would require a force of considerable size; and any interpretation that restricted the use of the militia to the American side of the boundary was an almost fatal hindrance to a campaign of conquest. If Canada was to be conquered, some new provision seemed indispensable.

If any man in Congress wished wholeheartedly for the conquest of Canada, that man was Peter B. Porter, of Black Rock, near Buffalo, New York—the "gentleman from Genesee" who had drawn Randolph's sarcasm. During the debate on the Volunteer Bill, Porter had given notice that when that bill had been disposed of, he would introduce a resolution looking to the organization of a Provisional Army of 20,000 men, to be formed from both regulars and volunteers and used at the President's discretion, without or within the national boundaries. Such an army would remedy both the shortage of troops caused by failure to recruit the regular army, and the doubt about the availability of the ordinary volunteers. It appears to have been the most practical suggestion offered for a force which could actually and promptly effect the reduction of Canada. Porter himself spoke in support of this resolution,[95] and without debate it was put to vote February 18 and lost by a vote of 49 to 58.[96]

---

[91] Adams, *John Randolph*, p. 290.
[92] For Monroe's explanation of the probable working of the Army Bill, see below, pp. 159–160.
[93] *Annals of Congress*, 12 Cong., I, 727 ff.

[94] Jackson to the Secretary of War, January, 1813. Parton, *Andrew Jackson*, I, 372.
[95] *Annals of Cong.*, 12 Cong., I, 1058–1069.
[96] *Ibid.*, p. 1069.

The defeat of the Provisional Army proposal was serious, but more serious and far more significant was the alignment of states by which it was defeated. The resolution was supported by Vermont, New York, Pennsylvania, Ohio, Tennessee, and Maryland. Against it were Massachusetts, Connecticut, Rhode Island, Delaware, New Jersey, North and South Carolina, and Georgia; while New Hampshire, Kentucky, and Virginia were evenly divided. In other words, those states having a direct interest in the acquisition of Canada—the states of the northwestern border—voted for the resolution, while an almost solid South joined with Federalist New England to defeat it. Put in another way, not a state south of the Potomac and east of the Alleghenies voted for the resolution; not a state bordering Canadian territory (if we except Massachusetts with her district of Maine) voted against it. More significant still was the defection of a group of southern war men—all of them in the front rank of the war party—Desha of Kentucky, Troup and Bibb of Georgia, Cheves and Lowndes of South Carolina and Grundy of Tennessee—the last as if frightened by his own recent prophecy—the prospect of too great an addition to the northern scale. Whatever the actual military value of Porter's proposal, it appealed to those men and sections having the most obvious interest in a successful invasion of Canada. Its defeat by southern votes indicates that Randolph's speeches had had weight and that Southerners feared they were about to pay too high a price for having their way in the Floridas.

More than two months later southern Republicans remained in the same doubtful position toward the conquest of Canada—at least if we may believe a bit of cautious testimony from one of the more moderate Federalists, Senator Bayard of Delaware.

"Judging from the course of conversation," wrote Bayard in May, "it would seem that the plan of the war is changing. The Western and Southern Gentlemen are alarmed at a point very seriously insisted upon by the Northern—that in case Canada is conquered it shall be divided into states and inalienably incorporated into the Union. You will see the great and permanent weight which such an event would throw into the northern scale. No proposition could have been more frightful to the southern men, and it seems that they had never thought of what they were to do with Canada before, in case they conquered the country, but they prefer that Canada should remain a British Province rather than become States of America. The consequence has been that they now begin to talk of maritime war, and of the ocean being the only place where G[reat] Britain is tangible. What I am now telling you is not an affair generally or publicly spoken of. It has existed but a short time and passes as yet in whispers and a semi-confidential way. I am inclined to think it true and likely to produce important results."[97]

The most active man in pressing the point mentioned by Bayard—that Canada if conquered must be retained—was John A. Harper of New Hampshire. Less than two weeks after the date of Bayard's letter, Harper wrote to the New Hampshire executive a forecast of the opening moves of the war. Among them, he thought, would be "an address to the people of Canada that they shall be protected in their persons, property and re-

[97] James A. Bayard to Andrew Bayard, May 2, 1812. Papers of James A. Bayard: Annual Report of the American Historical Association, 1913, II, 196.

ligion, and that that country shall be incorporated with and become a part of the Union. Upon the last proposition," Harper continued, "I have had much labor. I have no idea of having a war for several years to conquer the British Provinces and then surrender them by negociation and unless we can have a pledge that once conquered, they shall be retained, I will never give my vote to send an army there. I have reflected much upon this question and used all my influence to have it effected. I am in hopes of being successful. Until I made the proposition I believe it was not agitated by any member of Congress or of the Executive."[98]

Harper's letter supplies the key to Bayard's. Harper was pressing for a pledge that Canada should be retained. The southern members were reluctant—"I have had much labor," said Harper. We may piece out the story with some ex-

pressions in a speech of Senator Hunter of Rhode Island in the following winter. "The declaration that Canada should be conquered and retained," according to Hunter's story, "was the exacted pledge of the Northern men who voted for the war." The wording is noticeably similar to Harper's and indicates that Harper secured his object. But Senator Hunter also related how it was managed. The terms of the bargain, he declared, were "an enlargement and arrondissement of the territory at the two extremities: a fair division of the spoil," and he added that the southern men had taken the position: "We consent that you may conquer Canada, permit us to conquer Florida."[99]

Senator Hunter was a Federalist, and his testimony relative to Republican logrolling is to be received with caution, but this statement fits so neatly with the known situation that we cannot disregard it.

[98] Harper to Plumer, May 13, 1812. *William Plumer Letters*, MSS., 1809–1815, pp. 293 ff.

[99] *Annals of Congress*, 13 Cong., I, 528.

George Rogers Taylor: AGRARIAN DISCONTENT IN THE MISSISSIPPI VALLEY PRECEDING THE WAR OF 1812

THE settlers in the new states and territories west of the Appalachians gave vital support first to the Embargo Act of December 1807 and the succeeding attempts at peaceful coercion of the European belligerents and then to the declaration of war against England in June 1812. The importance of this frontier sentiment has long been recognized. The purpose of this study is to explore its economic basis.

In his policy of commercial coercion

President Jefferson received no more faithful support than that which came from western congressmen. Almost to a man, they voted for the original act of December, 1807, which placed a general embargo on foreign trade and they loyally backed the numerous measures which followed to make its operation effective. When, in November, 1808, the House of Representatives by the very close count of fifty-six to fifty-eight voted to continue the measure in effect, the

Reprinted by permission from *The Journal of Political Economy*, XXXIX (August 1931), 486–505. Published by the University of Chicago Press. A few minor changes have been made by the author.

western members were solidly with the majority.[1] And the next spring, when others weakened, western congressmen stood out for the continuance of the embargo, or, failing that, for the adoption of a non-intercourse act. A westerner, George W. Campbell of Tennessee, was one of the Senate leaders who held out most firmly against any loosening of commercial restrictions.[2]

On the whole, the citizens of the western states were just as enthusiastic for commercial restrictions as their representatives in Congress. Yet some frontier opposition did appear. At Pittsburgh and Presque Isle (Erie), in Pennsylvania and in parts of Ohio where some Federalism still survived (e.g., Dayton and Chillicothe), newspaper writers vigorously attacked the measure.[3] In Kentucky, the *Western World* of Frankfort, a paper with an extremely small following, was the only one in the state antagonistic to the embargo.[4] As might be expected from the presence of commercial and shipping interests, some active disapproval appeared at New Orleans, where at least two of the newspapers attacked the measure.[5] Even there the group opposed to the embargo appears to have

been but a small minority. Its size, however, may have been minimized by the intensely partisan Governor Claiborne, who wrote to Madison: "Two or three British Factors, and some violent Federalists censure the Embargo, but the better informed, and worthy part of Society, appears highly to approve the measure."[6]

Despite the opposition noted above, the frontier was, on the whole, as favorable to the embargo as its representatives in Congress. The commercial boycott had been successfully used against England in our earlier struggles, and it now seemed to westerners a natural and powerful weapon.[7] State legislatures, local political leaders, and public meetings expressed their enthusiastic approval.[8] Most western newspapers printed articles which ardently championed the embargo.[9] Opinion was so united in its fa-

---

[1] *Annals of Congress*, 10 Cong., 2 Sess., p. 500.

[2] See for example, *ibid.*, pp. 1475–87, 1499, and 1541. Matthew Lyon, of Kentucky was the only western representative in Congress who opposed the embargo and deprecated talk of war with England. *Annals of Congress*, 10 Cong., 1 Sess., p. 1222, and 2 Sess., pp. 1504–5. In spite of his early services to his party, his constituents were unwilling to have such a representative, and August 18, 1810, the Lexington *Reporter* announced that "the apostate Lyon" had failed of re-election. See also the *Reporter* (Lexington, Kentucky) for July 1, 1809.

[3] On Federalism in Ohio before the War of 1812, see Homer C. Hockett, *Western Influences on Political Parties to 1825*, pp. 54–62.

[4] In attacking the embargo the opposition press commonly claimed that the Democrats were ruining the country in an attempt to help the French.

[5] *La lanterne magique* and the *Louisiana Gazette*.

[6] Claiborne to Madison, New Orleans, June 8, 1808, D. Rowland, ed., *Official Letter Books of W. C. C. Claiborne*, IV, 176. The suggestion in a New Orleans paper that the people of Orleans Territory were opposed to the restrictions on trade brought a vigorous denial in the *Courrier de la Louisiane* for June 3, 1808.

[7] In what was perhaps the first book of a political character printed in the Trans-Appalachian region, Allan B. Magruder advocated the so-called "Chinese policy" and expressed the belief that foreign nations could best be coerced by depriving them of the benefits of commerce with us. *Political, Commercial and Moral Reflections on the Late Cession of Louisiana to the United States* (Lexington, 1803), pp. 56–65. The importance which the frontiersmen attached to foreign relations may be illustrated by the assertion of a Kentucky farmer that ". . . if our relations with foreign countries go on well, we are likely to have good markets at home, especially during the continuance of a European War." *American Republic* (Frankfort, Kentucky), June 21, 1811.

[8] See, for example, Mann Butler, *A History of the Commonwealth of Kentucky* (Louisville, 1834), p. 330; *Acts of Ohio*, 7 Ass., 1 Sess., pp. 223–24; *Scioto Gazette* (Chillicothe, Ohio), February 13, 1809; *Acts of Kentucky*, 17 Ass., 1 Sess., p. 129; *Reporter* (Washington, Pennsylvania), December 19, 1808; and the *Carthage Gazette* (Carthage, Tennessee), February 6, 1809.

[9] *Western Sun* (Vincennes), August 13, 1808; *Mississippi Messenger* (Natchez), February 4 and

vor in Tennessee as to call forth the following statement: "We never witnessed a greater unanimity to prevail in any considerable district of country, and relative to any important question, than now prevails throughout the state of Tennessee respecting the measures of the General Government. The voice of approbation is universal."[10] Two months after the measure had been superseded by the Non-Intercourse Act, they were still drinking toasts to it in Vincennes.[11] Perhaps at that distant frontier outpost they had not yet learned of its repeal.

Two writers, L. M. Sears and W. W. Jennings, have given special attention to the embargo of 1808. Both emphasize the traditional hatred for England, and the former specifically denies the significance of economic factors. Approval of the embargo, he tells us, was the result of the "simple trust" in Jefferson which filled the hearts of southern Democrats. As for the approval which was given the embargo in Mississippi Territory, Sears regards it as the pure flower of the disinterested logic.[12]

It cannot be denied that traditional attitudes and party loyalty played a part in determining western support for the embargo. To some extent the westerner was playing the role of a good Democrat and supporting his president. In part he was acting as a good patriot and a high-spirited frontiersman who resented insults to the national honor either by France or England. The traditional

friendship of Democrats for France doubtless made the westerner quick to resent untoward acts by Britain and slow to see evil in the French aggressions. But these explanations are, at most, not the whole story, for an examination of western opinion clearly indicates that the support which was given the embargo on the frontier had in it a considerable element of economic self-interest.

The western farmer was quite willing to admit his lack of interest in the carrying trade. Even impressment of seamen, though to be deplored, did not seem to him very important.[13] But he did want adequate markets and good prices for his produce, and these he believed impossible so long as Great Britain restricted the West Indian market, forbade direct trade with the Continent, and placed exceedingly burdensome duties upon American imports into Great Britain. In the eyes of the western farmer, the depression of 1808 was primarily the result of the belligerents' decrees and Orders-in-Council, not of the embargo which he regarded as a highly desirable act, designed as a measure of retaliation to force the abandonment by foreign nations of their destructive interference with the marketing of American products. "Who now blames the embargo?" demanded a Cincinnati editor. "Who considers it a matter of French interest or procurement? Who does not allow it to be a *saving measure?* . . . The embargo was produced by the foreign belligerent powers." . . . They made its continuance necessary.[14]

In Congress western representatives made no effort to conceal their economic

---

March 24, 1808; *Political Theatre* (Lancaster, Kentucky), December 10, 1808; *Wilson's Knoxville Gazette* (Knoxville, Tennessee), May 13, 1808; and *Commonwealth* (Pittsburgh, Pennsylvania) March 16, 1808.

[10] *Carthage Gazette* (Carthage, Tennessee), February 6, 1809.

[11] *Western Sun* (Vincennes), July 8, 1809.

[12] Louis Martin Sears, *Jefferson and the Embargo*, pp. 100 and 126; and W. W. Jennings, *The American Embargo*, 1807–1809, pp. 201–2.

[13] *Annals of Congress*, 10 Cong., 2 Sess., pp. 204–6; *Reporter* (Lexington, Kentucky), October 3, 1808, and *Kentucky Gazette* (Lexington, Kentucky), August 30, 1808.

[14] *The Western Spy and Miami Gazette* (Cincinnati, Ohio), August 13, 1808.

interest in the embargo. Said Senator Pope of Kentucky, in stating the very core of the argument in defense of this measure:

What, Mr. President, is our situation? . . . The dispute between us and the belligerents is not about the carrying trade, but whether we shall be permitted to carry our surplus produce to foreign markets? The privilege of carrying our cotton to market, is one in which, not only the growers themselves are interested, but one which concerns every part of the nation.

He then went on to show that if the embargo were taken off while the orders in council remained in force, cotton would be confined alone to the British market and the price would fall to a ruinously low level. "The necessity," he continued, ". . . of resisting the British orders and forcing our way to those markets where there is a demand for the article, must be evident to every one who will consider the subject." In conclusion he added that if England did not change her course war might be necessary.[15]

When the question of continuing the embargo was again debated in the spring of 1809, much was said of markets and prices by those favoring a continuance of restrictive measures. In arguing in the House of Representatives against the proposed repeal of the Embargo Act,

George W. Campbell, of Tennessee, declared:

. . . though you relieve your enemy, you do not furnish any substantial relief to your own people. No, sir, I am convinced that, in less than three months from this day, should this measure succeed, produce will sink below the price which it now bears, or has borne for the last year. There are but few places to which you can go, and those will naturally become glutted for want of competition; and, in a short time, the prices will not pay the original cost. It will, therefore, afford no substantial relief. The relief, too, which it may afford will be partial, confined to certain portions of the Union, and not equally beneficial to the whole. Tobacco will find no market; cotton a temporary market only—for, although Great Britain will receive it, yet, as we have more on hand than she will immediately want, or can make use of, and as we cannot go to France, and our trade to the Continent will undoubtedly be interrupted by Great Britain, she has nothing to do but wait a few days, weeks, or months, and buy it at her own price.[16]

If the inhabitants of Mississippi Territory gave, as has been held, a completely disinterested support to the embargo, one must conclude that their delegate in Congress failed somehow to understand the position of his constituents. George Poindexter, the delegate in Congress from Mississippi Territory, wrote the editor of the *Natchez Chronicle* that nothing could be gained by removing the embargo, for British taxes and trade restrictions would so limit the market for cotton as greatly to depress the price.[17]

By the Non-Intercourse Act, which superseded the Embargo Act in the

---

[15] *Annals of Congress*, 10 Cong., 2 Sess., pp. 1592–93. The West was outraged not only that English restrictions should keep our goods from Continental markets but also that heavy duties should be levied on the most important of our goods marketed in her ports. A contributor to a Kentucky newspaper declared: ". . . the *tax* in '74 was imposed on the article of *tea* alone, & whilst we were colonies of that country—in 1808, it is imposed on *every article of our commerce,* and that too while we occupy the ground of an *independent nation.*" *Palladium* (Frankfort, Kentucky), November 3, 1808, from the *Western World.*

[16] *Annals of Congress*, 10 Cong., 2 Sess., pp. 1481–82. See also *The Mississippian* (Natchez, Mississippi Territory), February 2, 1809.

[17] *Weekly Chronicle* (Natchez, Mississippi Territory), December 14, 1808, letter dated Washington, November 12, 1808.

spring of 1809, direct trade with England and France and their colonies was prohibited. Although there was nothing now to stop an indirect trade with England, the British orders in council still kept American produce from reaching the Continent. On the whole the West did not like the change, and their representatives were right in predicting that such partial opening of trade would glut markets with our products and bring prices still lower. Poindexter denounced England's attempt to monopolize world-trade and "tax the product of our farms when exported to foreign markets." He even advocated war against her if necessary, and did not hesitate to recommend to his constituents that cotton be shipped immediately to England via a neutral port so as to get a fair price before markets were glutted.[18]

The course of events during the summer of 1809 was well calculated still further to inflame western hatred for Great Britain and convince the frontier farmers that their surplus could never be exported at a profit until England was somehow forced to permit free trade upon the seas. Prices, although somewhat improved, continued low as compared with pre-embargo years. The Spanish West Indies were now open to American trade; but as early as June 5, 1809, Havana, the most important Spanish port, was reported surfeited with exportations from New Orleans.[19] Erskine's treaty (April 19, 1809) by which direct trade was to be reopened with England was, at least in some quarters, regarded with suspicion. If it should not result in opening trade with the Continent, it was held

that there would be loss for us and gain for England. The editor of the *Lexington Reporter* wrote:

What will be the price of our produce confined and concentrated totally in British warehouses?

Where will be our carrying trade? Why, British merchants and British manufacturers will purchase our productions for the mere expense of shipping and the duties and commissions to London and Liverpool merchants! *Our manufactures will be annihilated.* Britain will have gained a most glorious victory. . . .

What is become of the 100,000 hogsheads of Tobacco exported from the United States?

Will Britain consume and manufacture all our cotton?

No, not one tenth of our Tobacco—not one half of our Cotton; and our flour, our grain, our ashes, our staves, and every other property must center there, and be held as a *pledge for our allegiance.*[20]

In July news reached the West of the extension of the British continental blockade and of the new duties to be levied upon cotton. The *Reporter,* while bitterly attacking England, held that her insults were the results of our weak policy. "Submission only encourages oppression," wrote the editor, "and Britain will follow up her blow, 'til our chains are fully rivetted."[21] Probably this writer's attitude was extreme. Some westerners were inclined to look with considerable hope upon the Erskine arrangements.[22] But when, in the late summer of 1809, word was carried over the Appalachians that England had repudiated the acts of her minister, the frontier was thoroughly

---

[18] *The Mississippian* (Natchez), May 1, 1809, Poindexter to his constituents, Washington, D.C., March 5, 1809.

[19] *Louisiana Gazette* (New Orleans), June 27, 1809.

[20] May 13, 1809; italics in the original text.

[21] Lexington, Kentucky, July 1, 1809.

[22] Johnson of Kentucky, for example, was one of the chief supporters of the administration in its negotiations with Erskine. *Annals of Congress,* 11 Cong., 1 Sess., pp. 156–61. But most western representatives were not very enthusiastic. See *ibid.,* pp. 187 ff.

aroused. Public gatherings were called for the denunciation of British perfidy. Editors joined in the clamor, and state legislatures sent communications to the president denouncing England and declaring their willingness to resort to arms.[23]

The editor of the Lexington *Reporter* was not slow to drive home the moral. In a long analysis of the situation he said in part:

The *Farmer* who is complaining of the low price of Cotton, of Tobacco, of any other produce cannot now be deceived of the real cause, he will not attribute it to embargo systems, or to French decrees, for French decrees were in full force when we so anxiously made the experiment of *confining* our trade to Britain, the farmers will see clearly that the orders in council prohibiting and interrupting all commerce to the continent is the only cause for his embarrassments.

. . . The farmer who wishes a market for his produce, must therefore charge his representative in Congress to cast off all temporizing. . . .[24]

The winter of 1809–10 found hard times on frontier farms and western sentiment more bitter than ever against the British as the chief cause of the farmers' troubles.[25] The attempt at commercial co-

ercion had failed, but Congress was not yet ready to declare war. Beginning May 1, 1810, commerce was freed from the restrictive measures of our own government. On the whole, conditions seemed on the mend in the following summer, and western farmers were busy harvesting crops which they hoped might be floated down the river to good markets in 1811. Some thought they perceived a promise of better times, while others saw no assurance of prosperity until foreign restrictions should be withdrawn.[26]

But, instead of improving, conditions actually grew seriously worse during the next two years. Wholesale prices of western products were below even those of 1808 in the year before the war. In this new period of general depression on the frontier, the northern part of the Ohio River Valley appears to have suffered less than other parts of the West. Frequent newspaper notices of the building of flour mills in Ohio and increased advertising by those wishing to buy wheat and flour indicates at least some optimistic sentiment. Also, advantage must have resulted from a considerable increase which now took place in the number of cattle and hogs driven eastward over the mountains.[27] Although some settlers still came via Kentucky or by the river route,

[23] *Carthage Gazette* (Carthage, Tennessee), August 17, September 1, and November 17, 1809; *Independent Republican* (Chillicothe, Ohio), September 8, 1809; *Reporter* (Lexington, Kentucky), September 9 and November 11, 1809; *House Journal*, Tennessee, 8 Ass., 1 Sess., pp. 147–49; *Acts of Ohio*, 8 Ass., 1 Sess., p. 347.

[24] October 24, 1809; italics in the original text. See also *Carthage Gazette* (Carthage, Tennessee), December 15, 1809.

[25] *Carthage Gazette* (Carthage, Tennessee), December 15, 1809; *Reporter* (Lexington, Kentucky), November 11 and December 30, 1809, and February 24, 1810; *Independent Republican* (Chillicothe, Ohio), February 8 and March 8, 1810; *Liberty Hall* (Cincinnati, Ohio), February 7, 1810. The plight of the settlers living west of the Great Miami River in Ohio may be regarded as typical. They could not, so they reported to

Congress, make payments on lands which they had bought because (1) specie could not be commanded, (2) laws for the relief of debtors made it impossible for them to collect payments which were due, (3) immigrants were no longer coming into the country and bringing money with them, and (4) there were no markets for their produce. *Dayton Repertory* (Dayton, Ohio), December 14, 1809.

[26] *Ohio Centinel* (Dayton, Ohio), May 31, 1810; *Kentucky Gazette* (Lexington, Kentucky), July 31, 1810; *Reporter* (Lexington, Kentucky), June 15 and 30 and July 14 and 21, 1810.

[27] *Muskingum Messenger* (Zanesville, Ohio), November 24, 1810; *Ohio Centinel* (Dayton, Ohio), December 13, 1810; *Supporter* (Chillicothe, Ohio), March 30, 1811.

the fact which now called forth newspaper comment was the large number of wagons bringing immigrants to Ohio which were to be met on the Pennsylvania turnpikes and on the Zanesville Road in Ohio.[28] Along with this new wave of immigration, land sales rose, though not to their pre-embargo peak. So, at least a temporary market must have been afforded for considerable quantities of country produce.[29]

In so far as contemporary appraisals of the economic situation in this northern area are available, they show little or no reflection of the favorable factors just noted. Dullness of business, scarcity of money, "poverty, disappointment, embarrassment," "the present disasterous state of our affairs"—these are typical of contemporary statements. Taken along with what we know of the price situation, the disorganization of the Mississippi commerce in the winter of 1811–12, and the fact that settlers on public lands were still petitioning for relief, the indications are that, although there was some promise of better times, the region north of the Ohio River was certainly not enjoying general prosperity in the year or two immediately preceding the war.[30]

Judging from the extremely low prices brought by tobacco, hemp, and cotton, one might suppose that the frontier south of the Ohio River suffered from a more serious depression than that to the north. The records clearly show this to have been the case. The Kentucky farmers, who had turned so enthusiastically to hemp culture in 1809 and 1810 that hemp had become the most important staple of the state, now complained even more loudly than those who produced wheat, cotton, or tobacco. There is hardly an issue of the Frankfort and Lexington papers which does not give voice to the despair and resentment of these unfortunate frontiersmen. In spite of public resolutions and even co-operative action to keep up the price by refusing to sell (probably one of the first efforts of this kind among American farmers), ruin was not averted and prices continued their disastrous decline.[31]

In western Tennessee and Mississippi Territory where cotton was almost the only sale crop, the plight of the frontier farmers was most desperate of all. Tennessee cotton planters were reported in the fall of 1810 as so discouraged that to a considerable extent they had ceased the cultivation of their staple.[32] An able contributor to Nashville papers wrote:

Ask a Tennessee planter why he does not raise some kind of crop besides corn! His answer is—if he were to do it he could get nothing for it—that he could not sell it for money, unless he carried it to Natchez or Orleans—and that was out of his power—therefore he was content to make just what would do him, (as the saying is). Hence it is undeniable that the want of encourage-

---

[28] *Ohio Centinel* (Dayton, Ohio), December 13, 1810; *Supporter* (Chillicothe, Ohio), March 30, 1811; and the *Muskingum Messenger* (Zanesville, Ohio), November 13 and December 18, 1811.
[29] *American State Papers, Finance,* Vol. II, *passim.*
[30] See: William Rufus Putnam to John May, Marietta, Ohio, March 15, 1810; *The John May Papers,* Western Reserve Historical Society Tract No. 97, p. 211; *Commentator* (Marietta, Ohio), April 3, 1810; *Advertiser* (Cincinnati, Ohio), June 27, 1810; *Ohio Centinel* (Dayton, Ohio), March 7 and May 15, 1811; *Western Telegraphe* (Washington, Pennsylvania), July 18, 1811; James McBride to Mary McRoberts, "Mississippi River, April 1, 1812," *Quarterly Publication of the Historical and Philosophical Society of Ohio,* V, 27–28; and *Acts of Ohio,* 9 Ass., 1 Sess., pp. 90–91, and 10 Ass., 1 Sess., pp. 190–91.

[31] See files of the Lexington *Reporter* and the Frankfort *Palladium* especially for January and February of 1811.
[32] *Western Chronicle* (Columbia, Tennessee), November 17, 1810.

ment forms the principal cause of the indolence of our inhabitants.[33]

This was written in 1810. In the next year conditions were, if changed at all, worse; and "hardness of times and scarcity of money" continued to be the farmer's story.[34]

As for Mississippi Territory, conditions there were also "very dull."[35] Planters were heavily in debt for slaves as well as for land, and in the autumn of 1811 they petitioned Congress to permit them to defer payments due on public lands because of "the severe pressure of the times" and the "reduced price of cotton."[36]

In Orleans Territory the picture was much the same except that cattle raisers in the central and western part of the territory and sugar planters along the river received fair prices for their produce. But cotton growers were as hard pressed as elsewhere. And business at New Orleans experienced a severe crisis in 1811. The editor of the *Louisiana Gazette* declared:

The numerous failures lately in this city, has not alone been distressing to the adventurous merchant, but it has in a great measure paralized commerce, by destroying that confidence which is the grand key stone that keeps the commercial world together. This city is young in business, we have but few capitalists in trade amongst us, and a shock of adversity is severely felt.[37]

Increased bitterness toward Great Britain and a renewed determination to force her to repeal her commercial restrictions accompanied the depression of

1811–12. But frontiersmen showed no desire to repeat the attempt at commercial coercion; past failures had shaken their faith in pacific measures. The new attitude is epitomized in the following toast offered at a Fourth of July celebration held at Frankfort in 1811: "Embargoes, non-intercourse, and negotiations, are but illy calculated to secure our rights. . . . let us now try old Roman policy, and maintain them with the sword."[38]

Although it cannot be questioned that this toast expressed the predominant feeling of the West, the existence of an opposition must not be overlooked. Two western senators, one from Ohio and the other from Kentucky, cast ballots against the declaration of war.[39] Letters to newspapers and editorial comments opposing a definite break with England are not uncommon in the Ohio and western Pennsylvania press. In Allegheny County, which included Pittsburgh, the peace party was actually in the majority.[40] Elsewhere in the Mississippi Valley, with the possible exception of New Orleans, where, as during the embargo, the *Louisiana Gazette* was outspoken in its attack on all administration policies, the opposition was of very little consequence.[41]

Taking the frontier as a whole, the predominance of the war spirit cannot be doubted. All of the congressmen from western states voted for war, and the delegate to Congress from Mississippi Terri-

---

[33] *Democratic Clarion and Tennessee Gazette* (Nashville, Tennessee), September 21, 1810.
[34] *Carthage Gazette* (Carthage, Tennessee), August 21, 1811.
[35] *Palladium* (Frankfort, Kentucky), November 8, 1811, from the *Baltimore Whig*.
[36] *Ibid.*, and *Natchez Gazette* (Natchez), October 17, 1811.
[37] March 7, 1811.

[38] *American Republic* (Frankfort, Kentucky), July 5, 1811.
[39] The junior senator from Ohio was not present. His attitude toward the war is not known. See *Muckingum Messenger* (Zanesville, Ohio), July 1, 1812.
[40] *Pittsburgh Gazette* (Pittsburgh, Pennsylvania), October 23, 1812. See also *ibid.*, May 15 and 27 and September 18, 1812.
[41] The *Natchez Gazette* of Natchez, Mississippi Territory, and the *American Republic* of Frankfort, Kentucky, were opposed to war, at least in the manner proposed by the party in power.

tory repeatedly showed himself an enthusiastic advocate of hostile measures toward Great Britain. Both the governor and the state legislature of Ohio took occasion publicly to approve the aggressive stand taken by the Twelfth Congress.[42] In a vote regarded as a test of the peace sentiment the rural elements in Pennsylvania showed themselves strongly for war.[43]

In no part of the Union was the demand for war more clamorous or determined than in Kentucky.[44] The *Reporter,* which had long called for war, now demanded it more insistently than ever, and the other papers of the state followed its lead.[45] Before Congress met in the autumn of 1811 the Georgetown *Telegraph* declared: "We have now but one course to pursue—a resort to arms. This is the only way to bring a tyranical people to a sense of justice."[46] And the next spring the editor of the *Kentucky Gazette* expressed the impatience of the frontier when he wrote: ". . . we trust no further delay will now take place, in making vigorous preparations for War. Indeed those who believed Congress in earnest, expected a declaration of war long ago. . . ."[47] The Kentucky state legislature, which had declared itself ready for war

at least as early as December, 1808, now insisted upon a break with England and condemned further "temporising."[48]

To one familiar with the situation on the frontier in 1808–10 it can hardly come as a surprise that, in the same breath in which the farmers deplored their ruined agriculture, they urged war against England. Both on the frontier and in the halls of Congress westerners now demanded war as a necessary measure for economic relief.

When word of President Madison's warlike message to the Twelfth Congress reached western Pennsylvania, the editor of the Pittsburgh *Mercury* declared himself attached to peace but if necessary ready to fight for commerce.[49] And at the other end of the frontier, Governor W. C. C. Claiborne, in his inaugural address before the Louisiana state legislature, declared: "The wrongs of England have been long and seriously felt; they are visible in the decline of our sea towns, in the ruin of our commerce and the languor of agriculture."[50] Perhaps the statements of the somewhat bombastic governor must not be taken too seriously. But the following by a Louisiana cotton planter seems to come directly, if not from the heart, at least from the pocketbook:

Upon the subject of cotton we are not such fools, but we know that there is not competition in the European market for that article, and that the British are giving us what they please for it—and, if we are compelled to give it away, it matters not to us, who receives it.

---

[42] *Belmont Repository* (St. Clairsville, Ohio), December 21, 1811; and *Muskingum Messenger* (Zanesville, Ohio), July 1, 1812.

[43] *Pittsburgh Gazette* (Pittsburgh Pennsylvania), October 23, 1812.

[44] John Pope, of Kentucky, who voted against war with England paid the penalty for acting contrary to the clearly expressed wishes of his constituents. He was defeated by an overwhelming majority when he came up for re-election in 1813. John Bowman to Stephen F. Austin, August 5, 1813, *Annual Report* of the American History Association, 1919, II, 227–28.

[45] See especially, *Reporter* (Lexington, Kentucky), November 2, 1811, and January 11 and April 14, 1812.

[46] *Telegraph* (Georgetown, Kentucky), September 25, 1811.

[47] March 3, 1812.

[48] *Acts of Kentucky,* 17 Ass., 1 Sess., p. 129, and 20 Ass., 1 Sess., pp. 252–54. For other expressions of frontier demand for war see for example: *Mercury* (Pittsburgh, Pennsylvania), September 26, 1811; *Commonwealth* (Pittsburgh, Pennsylvania), April 14, 1812; *Muskingum Messenger* (Zanesville, Ohio), July 1, 1812.

[49] November 12, 1811.

[50] Charles Gayarré, *History of Louisiana, The American Domination* (New York, 1866), p. 283.

But we happen to know that we should get a much greater price for it, for we have some idea of the extent of the Continent, and the demand there for it; and we also know that the British navy is not so terrible as you would make us believe; and, therefore, upon the score of lucre, as well as national honor, we are ready.[51]

In Kentucky even the editor of the lone Federalist paper the *American Republic* denounced foreign restrictions as the cause for the depressed prices for western produce. He differed from the Democrats only in that he blamed not England but France, and also, of course, the Democratic administration for the hard times.[52] But this editor had almost no popular following. His paper, which went out of existence in the spring of 1812, represented little more than his own personal opinions.[53]

When aggressive action toward England seemed imminent late in 1811, the *Reporter*, which had advocated war to secure markets as early as 1809, printed an editorial saying: "It appears likely that our government will at last make war, to produce a market for our Tobacco, Flour and Cotton."[54] And as Congress hesitated over the fatal step, the *Reporter* continued to clamor for war. In April a communication printed in that paper violently attacked England as the source of western difficulties and de-

clared that western hemp raisers would be completely ruined by English measures.[55] And the editor himself wrote in similar vein:

We are . . . aware that many circumstances combined to reduce the price of produce. The *British Orders in Council,* which still prevent the exportation of cotton, tobacco, etc. to the continent of Europe, *are the chief* —(at the same time confining every thing to their own glutted market) whilst those continue, the carrying trade will be very limited, and bear down considerably the consumption and price of hemp, yarns, etc.[56]

In what was perhaps the most curious and at the same time most revealing article to appear in the West, this same editor wrote:

Should those *quid* representatives and *quid* members of the administration support war measures after Britain has forced us into war, they support it only for *popularity,* and fear of *public* opinion. Not that their hearts are with their country—But with the British agents and U. States aristocracy.—But the scalping knife and tomahawk of *British savages, is now again, devastating our frontiers.*
Hemp at three dollars.
Cotton at twelve dollars.
Tobacco at nine shillings.
Thus will our farmers, and wives and children, continue to be *ruined* and *murdered,* whilst those half-way, *quid,* execrable measures and delays preponderate.
Either *federal* or democratical energy would preserve all.[57]

When it is remembered that the streets of Lexington were safely distant from the nearest conceivable point of Indian depredation, the editor's reference to economic ruin and the depressed price of commodities appears somehow more sin-

---

[51] *Time Piece* (St. Francisville, West Florida [Louisiana]), July 25, 1811.
[52] *American Republic* (Frankfort, Kentucky), October 4, 1811. Also *ibid.*, July 19, 1811.
[53] It is interesting to note that the frontier opposition to the war in western Pennsylvania and Louisiana emanated not from the farmers but apparently from the commercial interests in Pittsburgh and New Orleans, and that in Ohio it came from a part of the West in which economic conditions were least depressed and in which a similar Federalist opposition to the embargo may be noted.
[54] *Reporter* (Lexington, Kentucky), December 10, 1811.

[55] *Ibid.*, April 25, 1812.
[56] April 13, 1811; italics in the original text. Also *ibid.*, February 23, 1811.
[57] *Reporter* (Lexington, Kentucky), March 14, 1812 (italics in the original text).

cere than his dramatic reference to the danger of tomahawk and scalping knife.

Nor did the economic aspect of the situation fail to find emphasis in the debates at Washington. In the discussions there on declaring war, western congressmen repeatedly emphasized the economic argument. Said Felix Grundy, of Tennessee, a leader of the western War Hawks second only to Henry Clay: ". . . inquire of the Western people why their crops are not equal to what they were in former years, they will answer that industry has no stimulus left, since their surplus products have no markets."[58] And Samuel McKee, of Kentucky, expressed frontier exasperation with those who counseled delay, in the following words:

How long shall we live at this poor dying rate, before this nonimportation law will effect the repeal of the Orders in Council? Will it be two years or twenty years? The answer is in the bosom of futurity. But, in the meantime, our prosperity is gone; our resources are wasting; and the present state of things is sapping the foundations of our political institutions by the demoralization of the people.[59]

So much has been made of the youthful enthusiasm of the War Hawks, of their national feeling and keen resentment of foreign insults, that it may possibly appear to some that these western leaders were great hypocrites who talked of national honor but acted secretly from economic motives. By way of extenuation it may be suggested that national honor and national interest seldom fail to coincide. Furthermore, the western leaders made no secret of their "interests" even though they did have much to say of "honor." Clay demanded vigorous measures against England, declaring that through failure to fight we lost both com-

merce and character. "If pecuniary considerations alone are to govern," he said, "there is sufficient motive for the war."[60] Three months later, when writing to the editor of the *Kentucky Gazette* assuring him that war would yet be declared, Clay did not hesitate to state in a letter which was probably intended for publication: "In the event of war, I am inclined to think that article [hemp] will command a better price than it now does."[61]

Confusion has sometimes arisen from the failure to realize that commercial privileges were as essential to those who produced goods for foreign exportation as for the merchants who gained by performing the middleman service. John Randolph did accuse the Democratic majority in Congress of being the dupes of eastern merchants. But one has only to read the words of the southern and western advocates of war to find that their position was clear and straightforward enough. Said Felix Grundy:

It is not the carrying trade, properly so called, about which this nation and Great Britain are at present contending. Were this the only question now under consideration, I should feel great unwillingness . . . to involve the nation in war, for the assertion of a right, in the enjoyment of which the community at large are not more deeply concerned. The true question in controversy, is of a very different character; it involves the interest of the whole nation. It is the right of exporting the productions of our own soil and industry to foreign markets.[62]

Repeatedly this matter came up, and as often western representatives clearly

---

[58] *Annals of Congress*, 12 Cong., 1 Sess., p. 426.
[59] *Ibid.*, p. 508.

[60] *Ibid.*, pp. 599–600.
[61] Clay to the editor of the *Kentucky Gazette*, March 14, 1812, printed in the *Kentucky Gazette* (Lexington, Kentucky), March 24, 1812.
[62] *Annals of Congress*, 12 Cong., 1 Sess., p. 424. For the position of John Rhea, another Tennessee congressman, see *ibid.*, p. 637.

stated their position. Henry Clay left the speaker's chair to explain:

We were but yesterday contending for the indirect trade—the right to export to Europe the coffee and sugar of the West Indies. Today we are asserting our claim to the direct trade—the right to export our cotton, tobacco, and other domestic produce to market.[63]

Too much has been made of Randolph's charge against the War Hawks that they sought the conquest of Canada, and not enough of his declarations that western representatives were much influenced by consideration of their own advantage.[64] It is true that pro-war Democrats of the coast states hurried to deny that their western colleagues were actuated by "selfish motives."[65] But Calhoun's reply to Randolph is worth quoting, for, although apparently intended as a denial, it is actually an admission of the charge. He is reported as saying:

. . . the gentleman from Virginia attributes preparation for war to everything but its true cause. He endeavored to find it in the probable rise of the price of hemp. He represents the people of the Western States as willing to plunge our country into war for such base and precarious motives. I will not reason on this point. I see the cause of their ardor, not in such base motives, but in their known patriotism and disinterestedness. No less mercenary is the reason which he attributes to the Southern States. He says, that the non-importation act has reduced cotton to nothing, which has produced feverish impatience. Sir, I acknowledge the cotton of our farms is worth but little; but not for the cause assigned by the gentleman from Virginia. The people of that section do not reason as he does; they do not attribute it to the efforts of their Government to maintain peace and in-

dependence of their country; they see in the low price of the produce, the hand of foreign injustice; they know well, without the market to the Continent, the deep and steady current of supply will glut that of Great Britain; they are not prepared for the colonial state to which again that Power is endeavoring to reduce us.[66]

Not only were westerners accused of seeking war for their own economic advantage, but many held they were mistaken in believing that war with England would bring them the results they sought. Federalists and anti-war Democrats repeatedly declared in Congress that war would not open markets or restore the price of hemp, tobacco, or cotton.[67] These speeches, cogent as they often were, failed in their purpose of dissuading the frontiersmen from demanding war, but they are convincing evidence to us that the anti-war minority, no less than the majority which favored the conflict, recognized clearly enough the important relation of economic motives to the war spirit.

Non-economic factors undoubtedly played a part in bringing on the war. The expansionist sentiment, which Julius W. Pratt has emphasized, was surely present.[68] English incitement to Indian depredations and Spanish interference with American trade through Florida should be noted, as should also the fact that the frontiersmen sought every possible pretext to seize the coveted Indian lands. Restrictions on the carrying trade, even impressment of seamen, may have had some effect in influencing western opinion. No doubt the traditional hostility of

---

[63] *Ibid.*, p. 601.
[64] *Ibid.*, pp. 450 and 533.
[65] *Ibid.*, pp. 467–75.

[66] *Ibid.*, p. 482.
[67] See, for example, *Annals of Congress*, 12 Cong., 1 Sess., pp. 626, 674, 676, and 710.
[68] *Expansionists of 1812* (New York, 1925); and "Western Aims in the War of 1812." *Mississippi Valley Historical Review*, XII, 36–50.

the Republican party toward England played a part. Many veterans of the Revolutionary War had settled upon western lands, and time had not failed to magnify the glory of their achievements or to add to the aggressive ardor of their patriotism.

But important as these factors may have been, the attitude of the western settler can hardly be evaluated without an understanding of his economic position. He was, after all, typically an ambitious farmer who moved to the Mississippi Valley in order to make a better living. In the boom times following the Louisiana Purchase he had regarded the western frontier as a veritable promised land. Moreover, the fertile river valleys rewarded his toil with luxuriant harvests. But somehow prosperity eluded him. When, in spite of tremendous difficulties, he brought his produce to market, prices were often so low as to make his venture a failure.

We know now that the farmers' troubles were, in no small degree, fundamentally matters of transportation, of communication, and of imperfect marketing and financial organization. But is it unexpected that in their disappointment (and not unlike their descendants of today who still are inclined to magnify political factors) they put the blame for their economic ills upon foreign restriction of their markets and supported the Embargo and Non-Intercourse acts as weapons to coerce the European belligerents to give them what they regarded as their rights? And when peaceful methods failed and prices fell to even lower levels, is it surprising that the hopeful settlers of earlier years became the War Hawks of 1812?

A. L. Burt: ISSUES AND THE EVOLUTION OF CAUSES OF THE WAR OF 1812

[In May, 1806, Britain declared a blockade of the coast of the Continent from the River Elbe to Brest. Napoleon replied with his Berlin Decree which first proclaimed a blockade of the British Isles (a mere gesture since he had no navy to enforce it) and second announced that any ship stopping at an English port would not be admitted to a French port. Britain's answer to the Berlin Decree was the Orders-in-Council which extended the continental blockade, closed the whole French coasting trade to neutrals, and required all neutral vessels bound for the barred zone to clear from a British port, secure a license, and pay certain transit duties. As retaliation for these Orders, Napoleon stated in the Milan Decree that he would confiscate any ship which had submitted to search by the British, had paid any duty to the British, or had touched at a British port. EDITOR'S NOTE.]

GENERAL ISSUES IN THE WAR OF 1812

To understand [the French decrees and the British Orders-in-Council] we should remember that they accompanied the approach of the supreme crisis in the life-and-death struggle between the two powers which were then by far the greatest on earth. Napoleon had

From A. L. Burt, *The United States, Great Britain and British North America* (New Haven: Yale University Press, 1940), pp. 220–224, 242–248, 252–257, 297–313. Used by permission. For footnotes in full see the original.

come to realize that his position in Europe would never be secure until he subdued Britain, and she that her freedom depended on his downfall. Having had to abandon his projected invasion of the island kingdom because British sea power effectively barred the way, he perforce fell back upon the use of his land power to accomplish by slow strangulation what was impossible by quick assault. Taking advantage of the fact that Britain had stretched her declaration of blockade to cover a considerable length of his northern coast line, he stretched his declaration still farther and justified his action as a proper reprisal. He proclaimed the blockade of the whole of the British Isles.

This was a sort of fantastic and inverted blockade. Napoleon had no navy to enforce it, and his object was not so much to keep goods from reaching Britain as it was to prevent them from leaving. Because of this inversion, however, and also because of the wide extent of his power upon the Continent, he could undertake to enforce the blockade without a navy. This was what he was doing when he ordered the confiscation of all British goods and also, under pain of confiscation, the exclusion of every ship that touched at a British port. By depriving Britain of access to the European market upon which her economic life depended, he calculated that he could soon reduce the nation of traders and manufacturers to cry for mercy. Such, in short, was his Continental System which he began to enforce vigorously in the late summer of 1807. Britain saw that, if he carried it through, she was done. The orders-in-council were her desperate reply. She extended her blockade to every port from which he excluded her ships; and she turned back upon him the provisions of

his own decrees, declaring that she would treat as an enemy any ship which, without first going to Britain, sought to enter any port controlled by him.

The position of neutrals became impossible. It would have been much easier for them if they could have chosen to trade either with Britain or with the Napoleonic empire, but this was not the alternative that was forced upon them. The real issue was the Continental System. Would they cooperate with Napoleon in upholding it, or with Britain in undermining it? The question presented a perfect dilemma. A neutral vessel could not approach any European port that was under Napoleon's sway without being liable to seizure, either outside by a ship of the Royal Navy or inside by Napoleon's officials; inside, if it had touched at a British port, or had procured British papers; outside, if it had not. It was a choice between the devil and the deep sea.

Each belligerent was coercing neutrals to serve its own end; and as neutral rights disappeared under the combined pressure, each belligerent defended its departures from the traditional law of nations by accusing the other of prior violations and by blaming neutrals for their non-resistance to these violations. Neutrals, however, could not accept the self-justification of either without shedding their neutrality, nor could they offer resistance to either without running the same risk. Resistance to both was unthinkable. It was then more terribly true than ever that law is what those who can and will enforce it say that it is; and that the principle of reprisal, once let loose, may destroy the other principles of the laws of war. Indeed, the "laws of war" is a contradiction in terms.

Both belligerents this time flouted the

United States, and both professed eagerness to resume conformity to traditional law; but each insisted that the other should do it first, or that the Americans should resist with force the coercion of the other. Theoretically, the two belligerents were equally oppressive; but practically, legally, and psychologically they were not. Britain's control of the sea, being greater than Napoleon's control of the land, gave her greater power of enforcement. Much more important was the legal difference. Her seizures were made at sea and therefore, according to her own admission, were a violation of neutral rights under international law, her justification being that it was a necessary reprisal against Napoleon. His seizures, except an occasional capture by a fugitive French frigate or privateer at sea, were all made in port and therefore within the undoubted jurisdiction of his own or a subordinate government. Strictly speaking, his only violation of neutral rights under international law was confined to the occasional captures just mentioned. Napoleon also struck a responsive chord in the United States when he denounced the orders-in-council as designed to establish the economic supremacy of England upon the ruins of the industry and commerce of European countries. Here we approach another fundamental factor in the growing Anglo-American bitterness.

Between Britain and the United States there was a mutual suspicion mounting to a settled conviction that each was using the war to cheat the other out of its rights. The British were exasperated by the paradox of their position. Never had they possessed such complete control of the sea, yet more than ever the sea-borne trade of the enemy was escaping from their grasp. As already suggested, neutrals were running off with it and giving it their protection. They were climbing up on the back of the British navy, whose supremacy persuaded the enemy to hand over this trade; and they were throwing dust in the eyes of British judges, causing them to release as neutral what was really enemy property. By such means not only were they expanding their merchant marine while that of Britain shrank; they were actually robbing her of the profitable prizes of war and also of the crowning prize of a victorious end to the war. In other words, their cupidity had leagued them with the enemy and drawn them into an underhand war against Britain. . . .

As British people believed that Americans were abusing their neutral rights to the vital injury of Britain, so were Americans convinced that Britain was abusing her temporary belligerent rights to serve her permanent economic interests and that in doing so she was furtively dealing a dangerous blow at their country. They saw her trying, under cover of the war, to monopolize the commerce of the world. This may seem absurd when we remember that their mercantile marine had enjoyed a phenomenal expansion through the war while hers had suffered a contraction; but we should not overlook some other important considerations. Britain was in a position to do this very thing, international law being what it was and the Royal Navy being virtually supreme upon the sea; and there was no gainsaying the fact that measures which she took to win the war also tended to benefit her own carrying trade and commerce at the expense of others. In the United States this further effect was bound to be regarded as intentional and not just incidental. The adoption of the doctrine of the continuous voyage con-

tained the suggestion that Britain would
destroy what she could not appropriate;
and the orders-in-council seemed to
prove it.

The American reaction appears all the
more natural when viewed in the light of
the past. Britain had laid herself open to
this suspicion by a policy which she, and
she alone, had followed for generations.
It was the policy of her navigation laws,
by which she excluded foreigners from
all but a corner of her carrying trade.
This application of the monopolistic
principle was purposely made to stimulate the growth of the country's merchant
marine, and was commonly credited,
both at home and abroad, with having
made it what it was—the greatest in the
world. Another object of the exclusion of
foreigners was to deprive them, particularly the Dutch, of their function as mid-
dlemen in international trade, and to
transfer this function and its profits to
England. Not unconsciously had she become the chief storehouse and clearing-
house of the world's commerce, or, to use
the language of the day, the great entre-
pot. She had attained a position where
she held the world in fee. It is not surprising, therefore, that non-British eyes
saw in the orders-in-council a new and
ruthless projection of the old and selfish
design. To Americans, of all people, these
orders-in-council were particularly offensive. The reason for their peculiar sensi-
tiveness lay in their own history: they
were being forced back into the dependence of colonial days. Once more Britain
was insisting that they should have no
trade of their own, that all their foreign
commerce must be under her control.
American Independence was at stake!

* * *

CAUSES TO 1809

On June 22, 1807, the frigate *Chesapeake*, commanded by Barron, left
Hampton Roads and stood to sea. The
British ship *Leopard*, Captain S. P. Humphreys, then lying off Cape Henry, also
got under way, and came within hail
about three or four leagues from the
cape. Humphreys sent an officer to the
Chesapeake with Berkeley's order. The
officer returned with a note from Barron
denying knowledge of any such deserters
as were described, presumably because
the order referred to them as British subjects, and refusing to be searched. Humphreys hailed and remonstrated in vain.
A shot across the bow of the *Chesapeake*
being also without effect, the *Leopard*
finally fired into the American frigate,
killing and wounding about a score of
her crew. After ten minutes or so, having
replied with only one wild shot, Barron
struck. The search was made, and the
four men were carried off.

Insult was answered by insult, and the
second was much worse than the first. If
American officials had intended to thumb
their noses at the British navy, at least
they had not invaded British sovereignty;
but the execution of Admiral Berkeley's
order was a blow between the eyes, and
a flagrant violation of American sovereignty. It was a hostile attack upon the
United States.

The country raged, and wild cries of
war resounded through the land. Not
since the days of the Revolution had the
United States been so united; and never
again was it so solidly opposed to Britain. Even the "most temperate people
and those most attached to England," reported the British minister, "say that they
are bound as a nation and that they must
assert their honor on the first attack upon
it, or subject themselves to an imputa-

tion which it may be difficult ever to remove." If Congress had been in session, or if the President had then summoned it, as he was strongly urged to do, there might have been a stampede into war; for it seemed that Britain had determined to provoke it.

The news of the attack sent General Turreau, the French minister, rushing back to Washington, which he had left for the summer. He went straight to the President and engaged him in a discussion of the affair. Jefferson told the Frenchman: "If the English do not give us the satisfaction we demand, we will take Canada, which wants to enter the Union; and when, together with Canada, we shall have the Floridas, we shall no longer have any difficulties with our neighbors; and it is the only way of preventing them." Nevertheless Turreau positively reported to Talleyrand "that the President does not want war, and that Mr. Madison dreads it now still more." He added that they would do everything to avoid it. If Congress should think itself bound to decide for war, its intention would be "crossed by powerful intrigues, because the actual administration has nothing to gain and everything to lose by war." Turreau's judgment was sound.

Jefferson kept his head and preserved the peace in this trying crisis. As a precaution against further incidents that might precipitate an open rupture, he issued on July 2 a proclamation expelling all British armed vessels from American waters and prohibiting intercourse with any that refused to depart. He thus administered an emollient for wounded national pride. He also dispatched the United States schooner *Revenge* to demand satisfaction from Britain, and he put off the call to Congress.

The shots fired by the *Leopard* were the onset of the gathering storm which blew itself out in the war. The magic of electricity might have exorcised much of the evil done on the fatal day of June 22, but the means of communication were then too slow. The British government, in defiance of a considerable opinion that the affair only served the Americans right and that war with the United States would be good for England, was anxious to expiate the grave wrong committed by Berkeley. It disavowed the action and it denied the principle. It had not claimed, and would not claim, the right to search ships of war. It recalled the admiral; and it was willing to indemnify the wounded and the families of the killed, as well as to restore the abducted seamen still in custody. Such was the basis on which the affair was finally liquidated, but not until long afterwards.

One of the conditions demanded by the instructions entrusted to the *Revenge* was a final settlement of the impressment issue. As "security for the future," Monroe was to insist upon a British renunciation for which, if necessary, he might promise the return of deserters. Innocent as this demand might seem in Washington, it naturally appeared as blackmail in London. The United States was trying a game which only powers prepared for war can play successfully. The British government decided to call the American hand. If there was to be any settlement of the *Chesapeake* affair, it must be without any consideration of this extraneous issue on which a deadlock had already been reached. In September the cabinet flatly refused to negotiate on Monroe's terms; in October it issued a proclamation reinforcing the right of search to recover British seamen, which was interpreted in the United States as adding insult to injury; and in November it dispatched a special envoy to Washington with instructions to settle the affair there without any reference to the question of impressments. Arriving at the end of the year, he found the American government willing to exclude it from the discussion; but then he discovered that the discussion could not be opened for another reason. He had also to require, as a preliminary, the recall of the President's proclamation closing the ports. This precautionary measure may have prevented some irritating incidents, but it certainly produced an irritating situation, to which the British squadron in the Chesapeake contributed not a little by defying the order to depart. By this time, however, these ships were gone, much to the relief of Madison, who had intimated to Erskine that British orders for their withdrawal must precede any discussion in Washington. But the British complaint remained. To withhold from all armed vessels of Britain a hospitality continued to those of her enemy was an unfriendly act bordering on hostility. The American Secretary of State and the English emissary had a nice wrangle over the point until the former offered, and the latter refused, to compromise by making the signature of the recall coincide with the signature of the reparation settlement. Thus the negotiation ended before it began.

Both sides were to blame for their failure to meet, and therefore for the *Chesapeake* incident's remaining an open sore. But the effect of their failure should not be overdrawn. Before the negotiation stuck on the second snag in Washington, other influences had complicated the Anglo-American quarrel; and even before the first snag blocked discussion in London, the spark struck at sea had blown inland and there had started a sort of underground fire. Because this fire has sometimes been regarded as one of the causes of the War of 1812, it calls for careful examination.

The *Chesapeake* incident, by raising the specter of war between Britain and the United States, quickened the dead hopes of the Indians and the dead fears of the American frontier, disturbing the peace that had reigned in the Old Northwest for more than a decade. Again the red man looked to their old "white father" [Britain] for salvation from advancing American settlement; and again the Americans saw the guilty hand of Britain behind a savage threat to their pioneer settlements. From out on the Wabash, Governor Harrison of Indiana Territory reported on September 5, 1807, that the Indian attack was only waiting for the signal from British agents. For some time he had been watching the spreading influence of that curious Shawnee leader known as the Prophet, and now he was sure that the British were employing this "vile instrument" to rouse the Indians against the United States. His was only one of many such accusations which were believed in Washington. Madison soon told Erskine that the government had "irrefragible proof" that the British were back at their old game. As a matter of fact, the one-eyed Shawnee monster was plotting against the Americans, and the vanquished tribes were ripening for a new war on their own account; but the British authorities had then no hand in fomenting this movement in the western forests.

The British authorities had actually been neglecting the red men. During the years of quiet following Jay's Treaty, there seemed no point in cultivating the old attachment. Indian presents were cut down and the Indian Department in Canada was allowed to run down. That was the situation when the international crisis burst upon the Western World. The effect upon the American Republic is well known, but the repercussion in the two British provinces adjoining on the north has received too little attention.

The news of the attack on the *Chesapeake* reached Canada in July through the United States, bringing with it the hot blast of American opinion crying for war on Britain. According to reports from south of the line, every American town formed an association to attack the neighboring British provinces. It seemed that hostilities might break out at any time, if they had not already begun, and there was no doubt whatever that war would mean an American invasion. The acting commander-in-chief, Colonel Isaac Brock, was greatly alarmed, for he knew that the country was totally unprepared for the danger. He feared that all might be lost with Quebec. Its fortifications were seriously defective, and he had no force with which to prevent the Americans from closing in upon it. He had no thought for anything but a desperate defense, and the octogenarian who was then temporarily administering the government of the lower province exasperated him by refusing to see the necessity for rushing improvements in the works and for calling out the militia. In a much more exposed position was Upper Canada, under Lieutenant Governor Francis Gore. Early in September he ran down to Montreal to meet Brock, his old friend and once his fellow officer, from whom he sought aid and advice. But Brock could spare only 4,000 stand of arms and declined all further responsibility for arrangements in the upper province.

The war scare was soon intensified by the receipt of a letter from Admiral Berkeley in Halifax, later confirmed by a similar one from Erskine in Philadelphia. It was a circular informing the administrators of the various colonies that an American ultimatum had been sent to London and that hostilities were almost, if not quite, inevitable. It reached Quebec on September 16 and York on October 1. As a result of this startling message, Brock got some cooperation from the civil government, but this need not be detailed here because it was solely concerned with arming Lower Canada. Of more interest is Gore's report from York, the present Toronto, for if there was any tampering with red men on American soil, Gore was responsible for it. The only political contact which the British had with the western tribes was through the Indian Department of Upper Canada headed by Colonel Claus, who took all his orders from, and made all his reports to, the lieutenant governor of that province.

In a dispatch to Lord Castlereagh, the Secretary of State in London, written on October 7, Gore reported that, having been unable to procure a sufficient quantity of arms from Lower Canada, he was refraining from calling out any part of the militia, "that the Americans may not be made acquainted with our weakness." He also explained that, before receiving Berkeley's warning, he "had ordered additional supplies of provisions to be thrown into the posts of Amherstburg and St. Joseph's on account of the Indians who have neglected their corn fields in expectation of being called upon by the British government to take up the hatchet against the Americans." Here it should be noted that these two posts were the British substitutes for Detroit and Michilimackinac, and that Indians commonly resorted thither from near and far, even from the region of the Mississippi. Their coming and going had seemed innocent enough until the international crisis suddenly cast a dark shadow over it in the United States. But this letter by Gore shows that British influence was being exerted not to incite but to restrain the natives. They, he stated, would have "made war upon the Americans some time since" if it had not been for the "temperate and judicious conduct" of Colonel Claus and other officers of the Indian Department.

*   *   *

There came a time, however, when the protraction of the crisis turned responsible British minds toward the use of the savages. The object then was not aggression but defense—to parry the blow that the United States might strike at Britain in Canada.

*   *   *

In some respects the situation was not the same as in the years following the Revolutionary War. The balance of position and power in North America had shifted, Britain having become much weaker and the United States much stronger, so that it was now more dangerous for the former to interfere with the red men living in the latter. However, there was much less scope for interference. In the period before Jay's Treaty, this western imbroglio had been a primary cause of Anglo-American tension. Now it was only secondary, being released by the crisis which began at sea. Because this could not have occurred if the Monroe-Pinkney treaty had been ratified, and ratification was withheld because Britain would not yield to the American demand on impressments, the conclusion follows that the impressment

issue was indirectly responsible for this revival of the old danger. Indeed the more the history of these years is studied, the greater appears the influence of this fundamental issue. Yet it was not wholly responsible for the British hand's reaching out into the American West.

This trouble stems from the entanglement of British and Americans in the interior of the continent over the plight of the doomed red race, an international phase of the old clash between a primitive people and white civilization. Jay's Treaty may have made the best arrangement possible at the time, but it effected only a partial disentanglement. The remaining limitation upon the sovereignty of the United States . . . inevitably roused American resentment. The consequent friction, however, was merely a minor irritant that if left alone would pass away, because the condition which produced it was essentially temporary, though it did not finally disappear until after the War of 1812. . . .

The whole international situation rapidly became much worse in the latter part of 1807 as a consequence of French, British, and American action. The change came before there was any possibility of liquidating the *Chesapeake* affair and quite independently of it, though there can be no doubt that things would not have been so bad if that unfortunate incident had never occurred. The new turn of events grew out of the mighty struggle in the Old World, which then reached its central climax, and the initial impetus came from France.

Napoleon's smashing victory over Russia at Friedland led him to believe that he had completed his mastery over Europe and could therefore make his Continental System work the destruction of England's power. Having persuaded

Alexander to apply it in Russia, he proceeded to enforce his Berlin Decree vigorously in the rest of the Continent. His orders were issued in August, and by the end of the month the news of wholesale seizures startled London. There it became practically impossible to get insurance for shipments to the Continent, so that they ceased for the time being. Ostensibly in retaliation for the way Britain then struck back at him, Napoleon tightened his system on December 17, 1807, when he issued the Milan Decree. This announced that any neutral ship, together with its cargo, sailing from a British port or having submitted to British search had lost its neutral character and become lawful prize.

The British action which thus stirred his ire was the issuance of the famous orders-in-council of November 11, 1807, modified and developed by subsequent orders, declaring a blockade of all countries in Napoleon's system, together with their colonies, and condemning their produce as lawful prize. This was precisely the weapon he had aimed at Britain in his Berlin Decree. She claimed that she had a right to do to him what he would do to her; and at the same time she prided herself on being more considerate of neutrals, for she made a number of important exceptions in further provisions to be noticed presently.

Such assertions were delusive. There were fundamental differences between the two belligerents and what they were trying to do to each other. Napoleon would have stopped all trade from anywhere with Britain, but he could not; whereas she could have prevented all intercourse with the French Empire and its dependencies, but she would not. He could not, because he had no navy and she possessed a mighty one; she would

not, because she felt that her life and liberty depended on continued access to the European market, from which he would exclude her utterly by means of his land power. In one respect their sweeping declarations of blockade were alike. Both were dishonest, being designed to cover only a partial though effective execution. Her object, however, was the opposite of his. Hence her tenderness toward neutrals.

Britain announced that neutral vessels might pass with impunity through the blockade of Europe if they were cleared from, or bound for, a British port in the Old World. They would serve her purpose. The strong continental demand for her wares would see to that; and she revised her navigation and customs laws to legalize the introduction of return cargoes comprising goods of enemy origin for domestic consumption or reëxport. Another "concession" to neutrals was that of direct trade with enemy colonies; for the British fleet effectively isolated them from Napoleon's dangerous system, and the British government was anxious to avoid unnecessary pressure upon neutrals lest she lose their indispensable aid in European waters. Even the produce of enemy colonies might thus find its way to their mother country, Britain collecting equalizing duties to protect the produce of her own colonies. No concession, however, was to protect ships complying with a new regulation of Napoleon, by which his agents abroad certified that their cargoes contained nothing of British origin. Such ships and cargoes were to be confiscated.

The American action was the imposition of the embargo of December 22, 1807. This was before the news of the orders-in-council, and of course of the Milan Decree, had reached America. Of all the above European developments affecting neutrals, the only thing that was positively known to the government of the United States was that Napoleon had commenced to enforce his Berlin Decree against even Americans in violation of the treaty of 1800; and this information had just arrived. It might thus appear that the American action was rather precipitate, but no judgment on this point should be passed without an examination of the background.

Both Jefferson and Madison, as well as other Americans, had long cherished a comfortable belief that Nature had placed in the armory of the United States a most effective weapon that might be produced at any time to coerce an offending power such as Britain and France. Their rapidly expanding country imported almost all its manufactured goods from Europe, and it provided the West Indian colonies with supplies on which they were vitally dependent. By shutting this market and by cutting off this source of supply, the American government could suddenly release an economic pressure that would be much more telling than any possible military or naval pressure. It would also be cheaper than war. The confidence inspired by this homespun theory was so complete that, as already observed, the administration walked blindly on toward war without making any preparations for it.

From the spring of 1806 the nonimportation act had remained on the statute book without being applied against Britain, suspension being followed by suspension, even though the complex quarrel between the two countries was aggravated by the unsuccessful efforts of Monroe and Pinkney to compose it and by the order-in-council of January, 1807, condemning American vessels plying be-

tween enemy ports. But the *Chesapeake* "outrage" made any further suspension impossible; and when the last one expired on December 14, 1807, the punitive act was finally allowed to come into operation, over strong mercantile remonstrances. The exclusion of many principal articles of British manufacture hit producer and consumer on opposite sides of the Atlantic and widened the breach between their governments. This American blow at Britain was no sooner launched than a British blast hit the United States. It was the October proclamation on impressments, likewise produced by the mounting quarrel and further embittering it.

The conclusion is obvious: by action and reaction, the degeneration of Anglo-American relations was developing a dangerous momentum toward some new crisis without any assistance from France. If Napoleon had not provided the impetus mentioned above, the near future would probably have seen the United States giving a further twist to the economic screw against Britain, for such was the logical sequel; and Britain might have proceeded to destroy the American trade with the enemy's colonies by blockading them or by canceling her relaxation of the Rule of 1756, for such was the recommendation submitted by a House of Commons committee at the end of July. It would thus appear that Napoleon might have maneuvered the United States into war with Britain long before 1812 if he had scrupulously observed the Franco-American treaty of 1800, but his mind was set on crushing England with his Continental System.

It was in the middle of December, 1807, just as the nonimportation act went into force and the impressment proclamation arrived, that the *Revenge* returned with startling news from Paris. Napoleon was laying violent hands on American commerce! Consternation and confusion seized Washington, where men now saw double. Two great potential foes, instead of only one, confronted the United States. Though weeks were yet to pass before anyone in the country knew of the orders-in-council, there was every reason to believe that Britain had already struck back in some way most damaging to American interest. Within a day or two of the *Revenge*, some vessels arrived from England bringing London newspapers of November 12, two days before the orders were published; and these papers unanimously predicted some such move immediately. Quick action in the American capital seemed imperative, and there was no question of what it should be. Hastily Jefferson drafted, Madison revised. and the cabinet sanctioned a message to Congress calling for an embargo. In four hours, the Senate rushed through a bill supposed to have been drawn by the President, but the House required two more days to pass the embargo.

A twofold motive inspired the measure. American merchandise, vessels, and seamen were in peril on the sea, and elsewhere abroad, because of the predatory behavior of the belligerent powers; and therefore the embargo was necessary to preserve "these essential resources." This was the only argument of the presidential message and the only official explanation in the United States. Madison straightway assured Erskine, and instructed Pinkney to tell Canning, the British Foreign Secretary, that the act was purely a precaution and devoid of offense. It was not to be regarded as in any way tinged with hostility. These professions of innocence were repeatedly re-

newed, but they rang hollow. Here we may detect a certain likeness to the dishonest blockade declarations of Napoleon and Britain. Neither Jefferson nor Madison nor any other responsible American believed the embargo had a single motive. They knew it was also designed to coerce the powers that were oppressing American commerce.

* * *

CAUSES FROM 1809

[Jefferson's embargo, according to Burt, was a complete failure. It played into Napoleon's hands without forcing any concessions from Britain. It ruined the commerce of the United States and heightened antagonism between Jefferson's party and the commercial interests of New England. Burt likewise contends that the nonintercourse law which replaced the embargo in 1809 (opening American trade with all the world except France and Britain) was simply a gesture of desperation as was the new law (known as Macon's Bill No. 2) which in 1810 replaced the nonintercourse law. This bill of Macon's opened American trade with all countries including France and Britain but provided that if Napoleon should repeal his Decrees, America would return the favor by stopping trade with Britain or if Britain suspended her orders-in-council, America would reward Britain by curtailing trade with France. President Madison was fooled into stopping trade with Britain in accordance with this bill when Napoleon quite dishonestly pretended to the Americans that he had repealed the Decrees. Burt complains that: "The independence of the United States was being frittered away. The country was losing its self-respect, the most precious possession a nation can have, as it failed to command

the respect of the belligerents. More and more the feebleness of the American government's policy had been teaching these embattled giants of the Old World that they could trample with impunity upon American rights, American interests, and American feelings."

By the middle of 1811 a new British minister, Foster, had been sent to the United States with instructions once again to try to clear up the dispute between the two countries. Despite Foster's success in arranging a settlement of American grievances over the Chesapeake affair, Burt suggests that his mission may have been a hopeless one. Editor's Note.]

. . . The settlement [of the *Chesapeake* account with the British, November, 1811] came years too late, when it could no longer do any good. It deprived some Americans of a talking point, but that seems to have made no real difference.

The root of the trouble was still there, and though Foster saw it he could not touch it—the British impressment of sailors from American ships. This was what was responsible for the bloodshed on the *Chesapeake* and the *Little Belt*. At any time it might cause other violent clashes, and all the time it was producing little incidents which had a great cumulative effect. As Morier reminded Admiral Sawyer, and Monroe told Foster, it was ever feeding American bitterness against Britain. The longer the Napoleonic War lasted, the greater grew this evil for which there was no cure. Very naturally, therefore, the American outcry against it rose in a marked crescendo during the last year of the troubled peace between the United States and Britain. Some historians, American as well as British, have believed that this discordant note was artificially stressed, and for confirmation

they have pointed out that those parts of the country which were most affected by the practice, the maritime constituencies, did not complain. But this interpretation, which minimizes the importance of impressments as a cause of the War of 1812, needs revision.

In January, 1812, the legislature of New Jersey adopted strong warlike resolutions denouncing the "flagitious conduct of the rulers of Great Britain," and particularizing two intolerable grievances. The orders-in-council came second. The first charge was "the abominable practice of impressing native American seamen while in the pursuit of a lawful commerce, forcing them on board their ships of war, and compelling them, under the lash, to fight against nations with whom we are at peace, and even against their own country." Foster, a very discerning man in close touch with the political currents around him, likewise bracketed impressments with the orders-in-council as the two outstanding grounds of quarrel. Referring to the former, he reported home that the members of Congress "who are friendly to peace assure me that it is a much more difficult task for them to explain this point to their constituents than the orders-in-council." In another dispatch he wrote, "It is to be observed that the federal party, however they may for the purpose of getting into power press lightly on the points of dispute between the two countries for the moment, yet do not fail on all occasions to complain of the interuption of their direct trade with France and of the practice of impressment exercised by us on board American ships." A few lines later, he asserted that this practice "certainly creates more irritation than any other [difference] between the two countries"; and he repeated his favorite prescription for easing the pain. It was that the government in London should occasionally collect and send out batches of impressed Americans with some money in their pockets. These are but a few of many passages in his letters to London which show that he regarded the American outcry against impressments as both genuine and serious. There is still more to be said on this cause of the War of 1812, but it is better to reserve it until we have examined some other developments.

From all we have seen, it would appear that Mahan was right when he said, "Conditions were hopeless, and war assured, even when Foster arrived in Washington, in June 1811." Yet a whole year, all but a few days, elapsed before war was declared, and this long delay casts some doubt on his conclusion. Was there something more that was necessary to prod a lethargic country into taking the last step? Further influences were certainly at work in the United States to produce war, and these call for examination.

The Federalists, who had been more or less openly pro-British, began to throw their weight into the opposite scale. When Foster studied the state of political parties in the summer of 1811, he discovered that even the warmest Federalists were disposed to resist the British "pretension that, as a condition of the revocation of the orders-in-council, France would repeal her system so as to admit articles of British origin, when owned by neutrals, into her ports and those of the countries under her influence." This disposition was probably genuine, Britain's cloven hoof having been at last revealed even to her friends. But the startling change of policy adopted by the party in the autumn was admittedly a *ruse de guerre*.

Shortly after Congress assembled early in November, 1811, a Boston paper sounded a new clarion call, said to have been written by one of the leading Federalists of Massachusetts. "The alternatives presented to the people of this country are a continuance and more rigorous enforcement of the restrictions upon commerce, or a British war. The last is probably intended as a bug-bear to terrify the country into patience and toleration under the former." This seems to be a fair statement of Madison's attitude still, for his faith in the efficacy of commercial restrictions took an unconscionably long time to die. Having stated the alternatives, the anonymous author blasted the "withering experiment" which would reduce the people of the United States "to the condition of the Chinese." He insisted that there was only one choice, and that was war. The country, he said, "may probably" be defeated but it could not be conquered; and he strongly hinted that war would overthrow the administration and restore the "best men" to power. They would prosecute the war with vigor or make the best possible peace, the implication being that the Virginia dynasty could do neither. "It is then the duty of the Federalists to prepare for the war they have endeavored incessantly to avert."

Rallying to the call, the Federalists pushed war measures so zealously that they embarrassed the hesitant government and alarmed the British minister. In December he reported that it was doubtful if the administration possessed sufficient influence to prevent Congress from recommending an immediate declaration of war. Leading members of the party told him they would vote for war, and they shrugged their shoulders at his "observations on the strange and dangerous nature" of their game. They assured him that they would have a short war, a political revolution, and a solid peace. But the party lacked the courage and the discipline to play the game through to the end. Deserted by a considerable number of their followers, some of the leaders urged Foster to advise his government against any concession lest it spoil everything. Incidentally he did the opposite. At the end of January, 1812, he reported that the desperate tactics were being dropped. "Many of the federal leaders mean to push their support of war measures no further," he wrote home, and he added that the party representatives on the foreign relations committee, "although they have agreed to join with the most violent democrats . . . have explicitly stated their intention to oppose the resolution for war when it shall be brought into Congress." This is what they did in the end, and we may conclude that their earlier aberrations contributed little or nothing to the advent of war.

The publication of the Henry correspondence early in March came like the bursting of a bomb which threatened to blow the United States into war right away. John Henry was a charming and insinuating Irish adventurer who, after living for some years in the United States, moved to Canada and was then employed by Governor Craig as a confidential agent in the United States when the war cloud caused by the *Chesapeake* incident hung heavy over Canada. When the cloud passed, terminating his delicate mission, Henry sought extravagant rewards from the authorities in Quebec and London. When dejected over his failure, he fell into the hands of a French rogue who negotiated the sale of his papers to the American government for $50,000 and ran off with the money. The letters thus procured were turned over to Con-

gress and straightway published. At first glance they seemed to prove that the British government, working through the representative of the Crown in Quebec, had been intriguing with the Federalists to disrupt the Union. Great was the consternation in New England and the patriotic uproar in other parts of the country. But the bomb soon proved to be a dud. The excitement died down before the month was out because, on closer examination, the papers did not bear out the first impression. Even the United States government had been swindled.

Other Irishmen contributed much more to the Anglo-American quarrel at this time. Though we are accustomed to think of their anti-British influence in the United States as commencing with the mass migration in the middle of the nineteenth century, rotten potatoes were not at the root of the trouble. That can be traced back to the disturbed state of Ireland in the latter part of the eighteenth century, and particularly to the Rebellion of 1798. Not a few Irishmen then sought haven in America. It took another Irishman of contrary political principles to smell them out. This was the British minister himself. Foster found an astonishing number of places of power. "America is governed by the Press which is conducted principally by Irishmen," he wrote. "Binns who was of the Corresponding Society owns one of the bitterest papers against us at Philadelphia." He might also have mentioned Henry's successor as editor of the *Aurora,* William Duane, an American-born Irishman who had been reared in Ireland and deported from India. On the day after the British minister wrote the words just quoted, Randolph of Virginia said much the same thing in the House. "The war spirit is principally stimulated at this moment by those who have escaped from

wanted their alliance to parry the threatened American attack on Canada. Now the British authorities there did their utmost to check the hostility of these tribes toward the United States, lest it provoke the American attack which again menaced Canada. But the governor in Quebec and the lieutenant governor in York could now be sure of the native alliance if they should need it. American ineptitude, rather than British solicitude, had seen to that. The international problem was the disentanglement of British and American interests in the interior of the United States. Until this was solved, every strain on Anglo-American relations arising from other causes was liable to be aggravated by American suspicions of British intrigues with red men in the United States. The problem was baffling. No mere law passed in Washington could stop the British traffic with Indians on American soil. That was protected by something stronger than the violated guarantee of Jay's Treaty. The American government had to wink at this particular trade because it furnished the red men with the articles which they must have and Americans could no longer supply, thanks to the ban on intercourse with Britain. But there was another solution, one which had often been suggested in years gone by and was now urged vociferously in the press and advanced in Congress. It was war with Britain to drive her out of Canada. That would quench the native war forever! It would thus appear that the Indian situation in the Northwest was perhaps an efficient cause of the War of 1812; but it is better to suspend judgment upon this point until we have examined another development with which it has been associated.

According to a thesis which has been widely accepted in recent years, we cannot understand why there was a War of 1812 unless we look inland. This thesis[1] may be summarized as follows. The quarrel over neutral rights on the sea brought the United States to the verge of war with Britain, but did not do more than that, for the maritime constituencies voted against war. The force that induced the last fatal step was largely, though not wholly, an urge to conquer Canada. This urge was chiefly inspired by the determination to uproot the British-Indian evil but was also compounded of the old jealousy of the British fur trade and a new lust for territorial expansion that anticipated "Manifest Destiny"; and it found abundant "righteous pretexts" in the maritime quarrel. "By the end of the spring of 1812, the whole frontier country from New Hampshire to Kentucky was insisting that the British must be expelled from Canada." But the people of the Northwest might have clamored in vain for war if they had not found fortuitous allies in the people of the South, who were likewise impatient

---

[1] Julius W. Pratt, *Expansionists of 1812*, an interesting book in which the author tries to explain the paradox, "which apparently gave little concern to the older historians," of the United States' going to war to uphold maritime rights despite the stout opposition of maritime New England. He carefully explains in his preface that his work "makes no effort to give a full account of the causes of the War of 1812, but deals with one set of causes only. The exclusion from all but the briefest mention of the maritime grievances against Great Britain is with no wish to belittle them." Ignoring this caution, many readers have leaped to the conclusion, which he never intended to suggest and does not, that the traditional causes were of relatively minor importance and that the real causes of the war are to be found in the West. He admits, however, that he "feels safe in saying that without the peculiar grievances and ambitions of the West there would have been no war." This conclusion, I have been driven to reject. But at the same time I would like to pay tribute to the author for having made an important contribution to the history of Manifest Destiny.

to take Florida from Spain, the weak ally of Britain. This combination, which promised to preserve the balance between North and South by adding territory and population to both, brought on the war. This explanation is supported by the much quoted words of John Randolph delivered in the House on December 16, 1811.

Sir, if you go to war it will not be for the protection of, or defence of your maritime rights. Gentlemen from the North have been taken up to some high mountain and shown all the kingdoms of the earth; and Canada seems tempting in their sight. That rich vein of Gennessee land, which [sic] is said to be even better on the other side of the lake than on this. Agrarian cupidity, not maritime right urges the war. Ever since the report of the Committee on Foreign Relations came into the House, we have heard but one word—like the whip-poor-will, but one eternal monotonous tone—Canada! Canada! Canada! Not a syllable about Halifax, which unquestionably should be our great object in a war for maritime security.

Confirmation has also been found in the division of Congress on the war issue, "most of the navigating interests voting nay, and the interior, particularly the whole frontier in a great crescent from Vermont to Louisiana, voting aye," with "only a small majority for war."

There is more than one *non sequitur* in this argument. Does the voting of the maritime constituencies prove that neutral rights alone could not have produced the war? Their votes were divided, as a glance at the map shows; and the division would have been more equal if it had truly reflected the opinions of the people. Nor should it be forgotten that this was the part of the country that stood to suffer most in a trial of strength with British sea power. Much more serious is another consideration which we

have already seen. The American government had to champion the maritime interests not only in spite of their opposition but also because of their opposition. The commercial and shipping elements had been betraying the national honor. They would have sold neutral rights and the country's independence for selfish profit and sectional welfare.

The southern pressure for war is also misconstrued. Why should Americans want war with Britain in order to seize Florida? Part had already been taken without it, and the obstacle that seemed to stand in the way of getting the rest was the possibility of British intervention. Britain ruled the waves, and the waves nearly surrounded Florida. Moreover the administration's schemes for acquiring this weakly held Spanish possession were well under way long before the "War Hawks" flocked to the Twelfth Congress. The one reason why the South should welcome war with Britain to aid in getting Florida was to buy off sectional opposition within the United States by letting the North have its *quid pro quo* in Canada; but, as already suggested, this meant running the obvious danger of the means' defeating the end. The reports of the debates in the *Annals of Congress* contain no suggestion of Florida's being a motive for war; but they do reveal another material motive which has attracted too little attention. It was a strong one.

The planters were being badly pinched. "Our cotton is reduced to seven cents, and our tobacco to nothing," cried old Robert Wright of Maryland in the House. He denied Randolph's assertion "that our own restrictive system has undone us," pointing out that restrictions on the export of these articles had ceased and if they had been the cause the effect should have ceased too. "The price of cotton depends on the demand for the manufactures of that article; the English-made cottons depended on the continental markets, from which the British manufactures are excluded. The price of tobacco never was materially varied by the consumption in England, but depended on the foreign demand from Great Britain, which, by their exclusion from the continent, is almost entirely arrested." The retaliatory system of the two great belligerents, he said, had ruined the market for these American staples, and since Napoleon had revoked his decrees the blame now rested on the British orders-in-council. Wright put his finger on the sore spot of the South. This was the one section of the country that was vitally dependent upon the markets controlled by Napoleon. It was not a commercial region; but its very life was tied up with commerce. Here was a further reason for championing the maritime interests in their own despite. Maritime New England would have deserted the planter South; and the rural North would have done the same thing, for it was attracted by the fabulous price of wheat in England and the market for provisions created by the Peninsular War.

The voting of the frontier constituencies from Kentucky to New Hampshire also calls for more careful analysis. Another glance at the map shows that the unanimity was broken in Vermont and more particularly in New York. But if there had been no such break, the attitude of the members from the interior would be quite understandable without any reference to Canada. Practically all the members of Congress, no matter what part of the country they represented or how they voted in the end, admitted that the United States had just grounds

for declaring war on Britain. This being so, it stands to reason that those who came from the interior were least inhibited by the fear of consequences. Their electors had little direct interest in the sea-borne commerce which would be disrupted; they had no settlements which might be bombarded by British naval guns; and, if we except inhabitants of New York and Vermont, they were about as secure from a British military attack. This immunity was the common contemporary explanation of the pronounced bellicose attitude of the interior. It was also said that the western members saw in a war a lever to raise the price of hemp and of other produce which their people wished to sell but could not.

Though the Indian menace, which was played up by the Republican press, haunted the minds of some members of Congress, there is a good reason for doubting if it had any appreciable influence in bringing on the war with Britain. The seat of the native strife lay off in a remote corner. Relatively few whites lived anywhere near it, and they had no representatives in Congress. There it was openly said that Americans had stirred up the hornets' nest, and the aggressive character of Harrison's advance on Tippecanoe was so obvious that it was difficult to deny. A close study of all the debates from the opening of the session until the declaration of war shows that very few members, and they only very occasionally, pointed to the red peril or accused Britain of instigating it. If the old nightmare turned any vote from peace to war, there is no evidence for it in the *Annals of Congress*. In the President's historic message of June 1, 1812, recommending a declaration of war, Britain is charged most positively with "a series of acts, hostile to the United States as an independent and neutral nation," and after the enumeration of these acts, which are a catalogue of the maritime grievances, a short paragraph insinuating that there was some connection between the hostility of the savages and their intercourse with the British is inserted as a sort of afterthought. This is the only reference to the Indian troubles and it makes no definite charge. Apparently the administration did not consider the native hostilities to be a cause of war any more than did the majority in Congress.

The conquest of Canada was frequently mentioned in the debates, but the suggestion that it was desirable for its own sake was made so rarely that a reader of the debates might miss it if he did not look for it. Randolph's words which have been quoted above should not be taken at their face value. This Virginian stood out from among his fellow members of the House as the most persistent opponent of war. He denounced it eloquently, at great length, and often. If he really believed that the effective cause of the pressure for war was agrarian cupidity, rather than maritime grievances, we might expect to find that he directed his invective at this dishonorable motive again and again. But he did not. His words which have been so aptly used to support this thesis constitute only a short passage in a long speech delivered six months before the war, and there is hardly an echo of them in the records of his many other speeches during these six months. In the reports of what was said by all the other speakers who opposed war, there is equally little to support the startling charge he flung at the warmongers in December, 1811. Evidently it was not considered to have much point.

This conclusion is confirmed by a careful reading of Foster's letters. They reveal him as not only most interested in whatever was going on but also as one of the best-informed men in the country, and they do not even suggest that an urge for the conquest of Canada was a cause of the war. At the very end, during the secret session in which Congress passed the act declaring war, the idea did creep into one of his dispatches. He wrote that Harper of New Hampshire, a member of the committee on foreign relations, was reported as saying that "it would be advisable to go to war for Canada alone" and "he would be for never laying down arms until Canada should be taken." The British minister's only comment was, "It is supposed that this was a manoeuvre by which to get rid of the question of war altogether, as it would be impossible ever to get the House to agree to so great an absurdity." He was perfectly familiar with the talk of an attack on Canada, but he saw war coming as a consequence of what had happened at sea and not because of what was expected to happen on land.

This concept of the war dominated the discussions in Congress, and it was not the product of the "War Hawks." Erskine had described it before their party was hatched. It was simple, logical, and honorable. Britain had injured the United States on the high seas, where she was invincible. To challenge her there would be to court defeat. Britain had a thousand warships; the United States had not a single ship-of-the-line and only a half dozen frigates. A swarm of American privateers might prey upon British commerce, but a few heavy vessels of the Royal Navy might bombard American cities and even capture American ports. The only way to make Britain submit was to strike her where she was vulnerable—in the provinces adjoining on the north. Quebec might be too hard a nut to crack, but the United States could easily overrun the two Canadas right down to that fortress, and Quebec without the country back of it would be of little value to Britain. The small attention paid to Halifax is explained by the plain fact that it was beyond the American reach. The prevailing thought was that the United States was potentially supreme on land, as Britain was actually supreme on the sea. Each country had its own element, though only one had used it; and Britain would cease from her oppression at sea rather than lose her share of the land. If the worst came to the worst and, as one senator pointed out, Britain should get possession of New York and New Orleans, they could be recovered by an exchange of conquests. The conquest of Canada was anticipated as the seizure of a hostage rather than as the capture of a prize.

Why, then, did the war not come in 1811, shortly after Foster's arrival, when according to Mahan the breach was assured? Why the delay of a year? The answer is threefold. For one thing, the government in Washington was gravely worried by the possibility that American honor might also require a declaration of war against Napoleon. He seemed determined to ruin American trade with the whole continent of Europe; his minions confiscated American ships and cargoes, they were still burning them at sea, and they even impressed American sailors. Repeated representations in Paris brought no redress nor any promise of it. The President's temper grew very bad as he saw more and more clearly that the Emperor had been making sport of him and his people. Monroe was furious. In defiance of notorious evidence to the con-

trary, he tried again and again to persuade Foster that the Berlin and Milan decrees were repealed; and then he turned to Serurier and used this evidence to prove the opposite. The outrageous behavior of France was aired in Congress, where it found scarcely an apologist. Members who advocated war with Britain commonly admitted that hostilities against France would likewise be justified. In his opening message and again in his war message of seven months later, Madison referred to the American grievances against France. It is quite conceivable that, if the French Empire had been as vulnerable as the British, the United States might have made war on Napoleon too.

In the second place, the administration cherished a dying hope that Britain would yet surrender her orders-in-council and thereby open the door for an accommodation of other difficulties, particularly impressment. The discovery of Foster's impotence, which followed almost immediately upon his arrival, was a hard blow, but it did not kill this hope, for Monroe told him in the summer of 1811 that the United States would soon send a minister to London. The appointment was put off until it could be submitted to the Senate for confirmation, and when Congress met he confessed that the appointment had to be abandoned because the Senate would not give its consent. Still the hope was not dead.

The third reason for the delay in declaring war was that the country was absolutely unprepared to wage it, thanks to the sublime faith of Jefferson and Madison in the efficacy of commercial restrictions. Before the United States could begin to fight, an army had to be found and before an army could be found, special legislation had to be passed. This required time, and then more time was needed because it was difficult to find the men and the money. As it was, the declaration came long before the country was ready for it.

Though the President opened Congress with a request for war preparations, he had not yet given himself over to despair. Preparations for war are sometimes the only way to avoid it, and he seems to have believed that London might repent when it heard the rattling of the saber in Washington. The faint hope lingered through the winter and on into the spring, showing signs of life at the approach of every dispatch vessel from England. The end came on May 27 or 28. On those days Foster had several interviews with Madison and Monroe, and to them he communicated a long note he had just received from the British Foreign Secretary. Its categorical insistence on the maintenance of the orders-in-council, supported by new proof that the Napoleonic decrees were still the law, at last convinced Madison that further discussion with the British government was impossible. Thereupon he drafted the war message which he submitted to Congress on June 1.

Reviewing the hostile conduct of Britain only since the renewal of Anglo-French hostilities in 1803, the President made four definite charges. The first was impressments. The second was that British cruisers violated the peace of American coasts, hovering over and harassing entering and departing commerce. The third was the employment of "pretended Blockades" to plunder American commerce. The fourth was "the sweeping system" of the orders-in-council. He said nothing of the *Chesapeake*, for that account had been settled. Nor did he mention the contentious Rule of 1756, for this question had been liquidated by conquest. There were no French colonies left, and therefore there was no enemy colonial trade. Nor did he refer to the contract with France, for France had patently failed to live up to it.

Henry Adams has accused Madison of "inverting the order of complaints previously alleged," and he says that "this was the first time that the Government had alleged impressment as its chief grievance." But it is just as reasonable to conclude from a study of this document that the discussion of the orders-in-council was intended to be a climax of the indictment. In fact, there appears to have been no intended relation between the order of the charges and Madison's views of their relative gravity. He was proceeding chronologically. It should also be pointed out that he had long since committed himself officially on the importance of the impressment issue. When he was Secretary of State his instructions to Monroe made it the crux of the negotiations in London, and as soon as he learned that Monroe was completing a treaty without requiring Britain to abandon impressments from American vessels on the high seas he notified him that the United States must reject the treaty for this very reason. There had been no subsequent negotiation over the question simply because it seemed so hopeless. The blood it caused to be spilled while the two countries were nominally at peace is grim testimony of its fundamental importance.

The bill declaring war was passed by the House of Representatives on June 4, the Senate passed it in an amended form on the seventeenth, it was returned with the approval of the House on the eighteenth, and the President signed it immediately. . . .

Margaret Kinard Latimer: SOUTH CAROLINA—A PROTAGONIST OF THE WAR OF 1812

YOUNG Mr. Calhoun entered Congress prepared for a showdown. It was June 3, 1812, and the ambitious congressman from South Carolina would recommend war against England. The Foreign Relations Committee, of which he was chairman, had deliberated only two days on President Madison's message, but, after a forceful report in favor of war, John C. Calhoun presented a bill of declaration. A majority of the House followed his lead and on June 4 passed the act, the Senate concurring with some reluctance on June 18. Madison's signature, also of June 18, marked the official beginning of war.

The grievances against European powers for interfering with American ships and sailors on the high seas had gathered momentum in a continuous stream of events for more than a decade. The Jeffersonian policy of conciliation, restrictive measures, minimum armaments, and "peace at any price" had generally insured against violent ruptures.

Until the Twelfth Congress, legislation aimed at France or England had in reality been a jockeying of party strength in Congress. Although party voting was far from regular, the major portion of the Republicans and the Federalists debated hotly on the embargo and the succeeding restrictive measures. The erratic stands of the Quids accentuated the hodgepodge nature of congressional opinion as did certain courses taken by the New Englanders. Believing that the Republicans would never be forced into a war,

Josiah Quincy of Massachusetts and many of his fellow New England Federalists voted steadily for armament and naval increases in order to antagonize the administration. Quincy wrote to Harrison Gray Otis on November 26, 1811, even suggesting that New England stand for war.[1] However, when it became evident that the young Republicans in the Twelfth Congress had plunged their peace-loving party into just that war, the Federalists pitched their tents in the opposite camp.

Henry Adams estimated that only a third of Congress was in favor of war early in 1812, yet on June 4 the bill in the House was carried 79–49.[2] The crystallization of sentiment had been the work of an enthusiastic group of leaders in the Twelfth Congress who were responsible for a notable change in congressional foreign policy within the span of a few months. The story of the "War Hawks" is familiar, but still eminently impressive. It is important enough to warrant amplification and correction.

Of the five or six major "War Hawks" prominent in most accounts of the war, three were young South Carolina Republicans in Congress for the first time. John C. Calhoun, William Lowndes, and Langdon Cheves arrived in Washington with a motive in mind; they came if not pledged, at least committed, to oppose

[1] Samuel E. Morison, *Letters of Harrison Gray Otis* (Boston, 1913), II, 33–34.
[2] Henry Adams, *History of the United States of America* (New York, 1889–91), VI, 170.

From Margaret Kinard Latimer, *The American Historical Review*, LXI (July 1956), 914–29. Reproduced by permission.

the prevailing Republican foreign policy. These three leaders in the war group frequently initiated actions so far from the old Jeffersonian line that even their fellow War Hawks sounded some misgivings.

Calhoun made his real debut in the Twelfth Congress on December 12, 1811, when he spoke in opposition to the mercurial John Randolph. The subject before the House was the recommendation for armament made by the Foreign Relations Committee, which in the opinion of Mr. Randolph and many others had veered well off the Jeffersonian course. In an effective rebuttal, Calhoun presented ideas still further from the original tenets of the Republican party, which he nominally represented. "I know of but one principle to make a nation great," reasoned the South Carolinian, ". . . and that is to protect every citizen in the lawful pursuit of his business. . . . Protection and patriotism are reciprocal."[3] These sentences seemed almost to echo a phase of Hamiltonianism.

The second South Carolinian, Langdon Cheves, as chairman of the Naval Committee spoke at length in January maintaining the power of the President to use voluntary militia forces in time of war. Such nationalization, obviously anathema to old-line Jeffersonians, also appeared unduly risky to some of Cheves's belligerent cohorts. Later that month when Cheves requested an appropriation for twelve seventy-fours and twenty frigates at the cost of seven and a half million dollars, he was supported by a large number of the war group as well as the Federalists, but the bill failed

by a close vote of 62–59. Clearly prompting Cheves's individual efforts were the underlying objectives of the South Carolinians—an effective navy and its complement, free-flowing international trade. Lowndes of South Carolina, speaking on behalf of the frigates, well illustrated their policy:

The Constitution was not formed for the exclusive protection of commerce, but for the defense of all the interests of the United States. . . . But is it in this nation, and at this time that the profits of commerce are confined to the merchant? Your trade was, a few years ago unrestrained and flourishing—did it not enrich the most distant parts of your country? It has since been plundered and confined. Does the industry of the country languish? Is not the income of every man impaired?[4]

The concern of South Carolina with commerce became increasingly obvious. When the Committee on Foreign Relations in March, 1812, planned a ninety-day emergency embargo—information about which was supposedly to be withheld from public notice until passage—Calhoun opportunely informed Josiah Quincy, leader of the New England commercial interests. Eastern longshoremen were consequently set at work to load as many ships as possible and clear them from the ports, and undoubtedly the southern waterfronts were in the midst of similar activity.[5]

The joint efforts of Lowndes, Cheves, and Calhoun were directed in April toward a measure to authorize the importation of goods from Great Britain which had been contracted for before February, 1811. Having no success with this, on June 19 Cheves introduced a bill for the

[3] *Annals of Congress,* 12 Cong., 1 sess., p. 479. All subsequent references to *Annals* except where specified denote the Twelfth Congress, First Session.

[4] *Ibid.,* p. 886.
[5] For Quincy's report of the incident, see *Niles' Weekly Register,* II, 110.

suspension of nonimportation, and Calhoun hastened to its support: "The restrictive system, as a mode of resistance . . . has never been a favorite one with me. . . . I object to the restrictive system."[6] In essence, Calhoun was rejecting on the floor of Congress the major basis of the Jeffersonian foreign policy.

When Calhoun led his fellow congressmen in requesting a declaration of war, he was displaying not only the views of the three most aggressive South Carolina representatives but a real solidarity in the constituents whom he represented. True, not all eight South Carolinians in the House voted as a bloc on every measure. David R. Williams, chairman of Military Affairs, had been in Congress during most of the Jeffersonian decade and accepted in general such established party measures as restriction, yet he had always acted independently and as early as the Tenth Congress had looked favorably toward war. He spoke forcefully for the cause of armaments and resistance to Great Britain: "It has been said our Constitution is not calculated to sustain a war. It surely is not calculated for submission."[7] The other representatives, Moore, Earle, Butler, and Winn, had also been in earlier Jeffersonian Congresses, the latter two prominent Revolutionary soldiers. They belonged to a different generation from the young Calhoun, Cheves, and Lowndes, and their approaches to problems were similarly varied, but they shared fundamental principles based on the desires of their constituents at home. A majority of South Carolina representatives did support Cheves's bill for frig-

ates, and all voted for the added military forces. When the crucial vote was taken, South Carolina cast a solid eight for war. The two senators, Gaillard and Taylor, likewise voted in its favor. Kentucky, Tennessee, and Georgia, casting in the House five, three, and three votes respectively, were the only other states which were unanimously in favor of war with England.[8]

The "War Hawks"—primarily from the four above-mentioned states—were given special emphasis by Julius W. Pratt in his *Expansionists of 1812,* which set forward in 1925 what has become one of the most popular and widespread theories regarding the War of 1812. Basically, Pratt asserts that the Southwest and its war-minded leaders gave a major impetus to the war. Singling out the war group in Congress is highly significant in tracing the origins of the war sentiment, but the further direction taken by the Pratt school is more open to question: the "Southwest," including South Carolina as well as the inland states, is depicted as desirous of war largely because of an urge for frontier expansion and a concern with the Indian question. These basic ideas repeatedly occur in historical literature, most recently in a 1954 popularized account of the war, even though varying shades of doubt have from time to time been cast on the Pratt thesis. Not well enough known perhaps is the work of George Rogers Taylor in 1930 describing

---

[6] *Annals,* pp. 1281–1312, 1511, 1539.

[7] *Ibid.,* p. 682. Williams was a Charleston planter. See James H. Wolfe, *Jeffersonian Democracy in South Carolina* (Chapel Hill, 1940), p. 218; *Dictionary of American Biography,* XX.

[8] *Annals,* pp. 287, 1637. There were no negative votes from these states. Senator Pope of Kentucky, however, did not favor war and refrained from voting on the issue. He did not thereby represent the feelings of his constituents, because his action resulted in disgrace at home and defeat in the next election. See John Bowman to Stephen F. Austin, Aug. 5, 1813, *Austin Papers,* ed. E. C. Barker, American Historical Association, *Annual Report,* 1919, II, 227–28.

the dire economic conditions in the Mississippi Valley preceding the war and the resulting attitude of the western farmer toward international affairs.[9]

In A. L. Burt's study, *The United States, Great Britain and British North America* (1940), it is maintained that the War of 1812 was fought primarily for maritime rights; Burt discusses with thoroughness the diplomatic wrangles with Britain and France from the turn of the century onward, as an offshoot suggesting pertinent objections to Pratt. A historiographical article of 1941 by Warren H. Goodman gives a good progressive account of theories regarding the causes of the war, although it was unhappily prepared before the publication of Burt's work. Goodman does, however, make several elucidating observations about the Pratt thesis and takes successful issue with various of its aspects. Pointing to the need for much further investigation, Goodman concludes that the causes of the War of 1812 are still "singularly uncertain."[10]

Although South Carolina is included as an integral segment of the "South" and "Southwest" in the Burt and Pratt theses

respectively, little has been said specifically about South Carolina's part in the drive for war. Nor in the many studies of John C. Calhoun has more than scant attention been given to his basic stands in the Twelfth Congress. During this era, South Carolina has been simply catalogued with the Jeffersonian states because of its nominal support of the Republican party in national elections from 1796 onward, and Calhoun and his fellow South Carolina "War Hawks" are neatly fitted into the same package. Many of the ambiguities associated with "Jeffersonian democracy" are regularly applied to South Carolina, which did of course share in the countrywide liberalizing trends. Sufficient attention has been given to the formal rise of the Republican party to control within the state,[11] yet too often overlooked in this period of history have been the other factors which explain South Carolina's important relation to the war and which at the same time elucidate the state-centered aims of the "young nationalist" Calhoun.

* * *

South Carolina's agrarian economy was one of the major factors which drew her originally into the Republican fold. But it was the growing preoccupation of South Carolina with the international commerce necessary to make agriculture profitable that took her somewhat off the path envisaged by Jefferson. Attacking the traditional Jeffersonian international

[9] See currently, Glenn Tucker, *Poltroons and Patriots* (Indianapolis, 1954). The Taylor work appeared in two articles: "Agrarian Discontent in the Mississippi Valley Preceding the War of 1812," *Journal of Political Economy,* XXXIX (1931), 471–505; and "Prices in the Mississippi Valley Preceding the War of 1812," *Journal of Economic and Business History,* III (1930), 148–63.

[10] Warren H. Goodman, "The Origins of the War of 1812," *Mississippi Valley Historical Review,* XXVIII (1941), 171–86. Goodman's conclusion is based on the fact that nineteenth-century authors dealt primarily with military events and the twentieth century has netted only monographs on restricted phases of the question. No writer has attempted to "correlate and synthesize the various sets of causes," weighing the relative importance of the factors. Goodman makes an able suggestion of some eleven fields for investigation.

[11] J. H. Wolfe in his *Jeffersonian Democracy in South Carolina* gives a thorough factual discussion of this movement. Although the term "Jeffersonian democracy" has come into popular use, I question its preciseness of meaning for any area and especially with regard to South Carolina. Wolfe, however, is making in his title a correct distinction between the liberalism of this era and that of Jackson's, which South Carolina never accepted. See Wolfe, p. 286.

policy, the Republican William Lowndes said to Congress, "The interests of agriculture and commerce are inseparable. What is commerce but the exchange of the surplus produce of . . . one nation for those of another? . . . it is this commerce which makes agriculture valuable."[12] Such a positive stand was not unusual, for South Carolina never demonstrated a very close adherence to the national party. The local Republican group so well represented the interests of the planting-business community of the state as a whole that its standard-bearers received almost no opposition from the Federalists in elections for national representatives, and the delegates in turn exercised a notable independence and lack of partisanship in Congress. Edward Hooker's description of Wade Hampton, one of the prosperous upcountry Republicans, was almost generally applicable to South Carolinians: "In his politics he is, I hardly know what. He is called a republican; yet he certainly has many notions and sentiments which are more characteristic of federalism. And he does not hesitate to condemn openly, and unequivocably some measures of the republican party."[13]

Calhoun, Cheves, and Lowndes had come to prominence in this era of independent Republicanism and conservative political unanimity. Calhoun was from Scotch-Irish upcountry stock, although the holdings of his father put him easily in the category of "planter."[14] After early training at the academy of Moses Waddell in Georgia, Calhoun went to Yale, where his seriousness and sternness must have made him well fitted for Timothy Dwight's domain. This Federalist president had a pervading influence over the students at Yale College, and it seems unlikely that Calhoun was untouched by his ideas. Experience in the Charleston law office of Henry W. DeSaussure and formal study at Litchfield Law School in Connecticut under Federalists James Gould and Tapping Reeve contributed further to Calhoun's background of conservatism. In 1811, his marriage to Floride Calhoun, a cousin who belonged to wealthy Charlestonian society, gave the Republican uplander a direct tie to the older, more staid South Carolina lowcountry.

Calhoun was a lawyer in the Piedmont region at the time that the Chesapeake-Leopard affair provoked indignant public meetings in many localities. His first chance at public oratory came when he was requested by the Abbeville committee to write and present its resolutions denouncing the incident; shortly thereafter he was elected to the state legislature, and in 1810 he became a representative to the United States Congress.

[12] *Annals*, pp. 805–806.
[13] J. Franklin Jameson, ed., "Diary of Edward Hooker, 1805–1808." A.H.A. *Annual Report*, 1896, I, 847. Among other South Carolinians in Congress who acted independently was Senator John Gaillard, who broke from his party in voting against the Chase impeachment. Thomas Sumter consistently voted against nonintercourse and the embargo; he and D. R. Williams have been singled out as particularly nonpartisan spirits among the Republicans. Senator John Taylor, concerned by the depressing effects of the embargo, worked for less extreme measures; he was the real author of Macon's Bill No. 2, which did grant some relief. See Albert J. Beveridge, *The Life of John Marshall* (Boston, 1919), III, 218; Anne King Gregorie, *Thomas Sumter* (Columbia, S.C., 1931), p. 260; Wolfe, *Jeffersonian Democracy*, pp. 203–206; letter to Joseph H.

Nicholson from Nathaniel Macon, Apr. 10, 1810, in William E. Dodd, *Nathaniel Macon* (Raleigh, N.C., 1903), p. 259.
[14] Patrick Calhoun is credited with over 1000 acres of land and 31 slaves in 1790. Charles M. Wiltse, *John C. Calhoun*, II (Indianapolis, 1944), 17–23. See also Wallace, *History of South Carolina*, II, 386.

Langdon Cheves, also newly elected to Congress in 1810, had both upcountry and lowcountry connections as did Calhoun. He was born in Abbeville, a Piedmont district, and later became a lawyer in Charleston. The third new congressman, William Lowndes, was of lowcountry planting origin, and his attractive and intelligent wife was a confirmed Federalist, the daughter of Thomas Pinckney.[15]

Calhoun, Cheves, and Lowndes, Republicans with backgrounds strongly marked by conservative influences, expressed in the Twelfth Congress the conservatism which had become characteristic of South Carolina's "Federal"-Republicanism. All three were men of outstanding leadership abilities; and, when they made demands in the interest of their state, they also revealed a strong bent toward nationalization. Though nationalism can be the manifestation of both liberal and conservative movements, in 1811 nationalizing measures were definitely the latter. The conservatives during the Constitution-making era were the nationalists, and the South Carolinians were of this breed—conservatives in their desire to preserve the prevailing socio-economic system of their state. They sought federal power to protect this way of life.[16] Their nationalism was thus, in a sense, a sectionalism in disguise.

Calhoun, Cheves, and Lowndes were elected to Congress in 1810 with "reference to the critical condition of the country."[17] They were all in a belligerent mood, and they had spoken vigorously in pre-election campaigns. A clear statement of Calhoun's views on international affairs had been set forward as early as the Republican caucus in 1808: reviewing the struggle between the United States and European powers, he labeled the resort to the restrictive system an inefficient means of preserving American rights and pointed out that war with England was unavoidable. He later saw "in the low price of the produce, the hand of foreign injustice."[18] British minister Augustus J. Foster, who met the representatives in Washington, noted that the South Carolina members of Congress were "resolute," "particularly the younger Deputies . . . who seemed to have great influence and were very cool and decided on the propriety of going to war in order to protect the Commerce of the Country."[19] The South Carolina congressmen had a vital interest in the "Commerce of the Country," because on it depended the future of the prosperous economic developments which had taken place in South Carolina during the first decade of the nineteenth century.

By 1811 the entire state was in the middle of a tremendous cotton boom. The value and practicability of upland-grown short-staple cotton had become immediately apparent upon invention of the cotton gin and were demonstrated after the introduction of the gin into South Carolina in 1801; at the same time the demand for cotton went up as machine methods of manufacture became standard in England. When the slave trade was reopened in 1803, cotton pro-

---

[15] See DAB, IV, XI, for biographies of Cheves and Lowndes; also Ravenel, Life and Times of William Lowndes.

[16] Whether nationalization was a rightist or leftist move perhaps became questionable during the Jacksonian period. If one assumes Calhoun always to have been a conservative, his inconsistencies which appeared during the Jackson era have some basis for explanation.

[17] [John C. Calhoun], Life of John C. Calhoun (New York, 1843), p. 8.

[18] Annals, p. 482. For Calhoun's own description of the 1808 caucus at which he opposed the nomination of George Clinton for Vice President, see Life of John C. Calhoun, p. 7.

[19] MS Notes, Augustus J. Foster Papers, Library of Congress; see also MS Diary, Apr. 15, 1812, L.C.

duction proceeded at full speed. South Carolina doubled its cotton output in the ten years following 1801, producing forty million pounds in 1811; the state had begun to export approximately forty per cent of the total cotton exports of the United States.[20] As David Ramsay wrote in 1808, cotton "has trebled the price of land suitable to its growth, and when the crop succeeds and the market is favorable, the annual income of those who plant it is double to what it was before the introduction of cotton."[21]

The increased use of the Negro slave was of course necessary for the phenomenal expansion of upland cotton, and during these years a constantly growing num-

Charleston and Colleton the black population was actually much greater than the white, but here cotton and rice production had probably been expanded to the limit before 1800 since the percentage of slave population even decreased slightly in the period 1800–1810. It was the upcountry legislators who insisted on the reopening of the slave trade in 1803, for it was their region in which cotton and slavery were spreading. A look at the United States Census figures for 1790, 1800, and 1810 shows as expected a steady increase in slaves for upcountry districts, the largest proportional gain coming after 1800. The following are sample Piedmont districts:[23]

	York		Greenville		Edgefield	
	Slaves	Whites	Slaves	Whites	Slaves	Whites
1790	923	5,652	606	5,888	3,619	9,805
1800	1,804	8,417	1,439	10,029	5,006	13,063
1810	3,164	7,828	2,391	10,739	8,57/,	14,433

ber of farmers and planters acquired property in slaves. It is important to note, however, that in twenty-three out of twenty-eight districts in 1810 whites still outnumbered blacks, the popular image depicting masses of Negroes working on all the farm lands being far from correct.[22] True, in coast districts such as

When the upland area like the coast became a significant producer of cotton, South Carolina could boast an amazing unity of economic interest. Corollary to this economic development was of course the spread of political power into the upcountry and the resulting era in which political and cultural oneness increased steadily. This unanimity of interest, political and economic, exhibited itself under the name of Republicanism.

The enactment of the embargo by the federal government in 1808 exactly coincided with the full realizations of South Carolinians that the primary economic interests of the state were much the same from coast to hill country, that a continuance of the cotton-planting system was essential to all areas. The discomforts brought on by the embargo gave the state an even greater unity as both sec-

[20] The amount of cotton produced in South Carolina is an approximation made by Frederick J. Turner, *Rise of the New West* (New York, 1906), p. 47, based on a group of figures. See Matthew B. Hammond, *The Cotton Industry* (New York, 1897), Appendix I, p. 358, for total yearly cotton production and exports of the United States in 1811. See *Niles' Weekly Register*, I, 399, for exports of each state in 1811.

[21] David Ramsay, *History of South Carolina* (Newberry, S.C., 1858), II, 121.

[22] Schaper, *Sectionalism and Representation*, p. 392, gives a map of the enlarging "Black Belt" which shows a much greater preponderance of Negroes in South Carolina at this date. However, he lists no source. Census of 1810 bears out the above statement. See *Niles' Weekly Register*, I, 309.

[23] *Ibid.*, I, 309. See also Wiltse, *Calhoun*, II, 146.

tions were prey to the economic forces which made prices go up at the same time that profits decreased. The southern agriculturalists incurred constant expenses whether or not their products sold, but the traditional planting system had to be kept. Manufacturing had no chance to develop because after 1803 the capital of the South had gone into buying slaves; the area was already in debt to New England.[24]

The Charleston *Courier* reported on January 20, 1808, that cotton was down to twenty-five cents per pound, and on February 10, 1810, that it had fallen to fourteen cents. A contemporary observer reported that in order to make ends meet, the South Carolinians had to get at least twenty cents for their cotton.[25] One should note that the critical drop in price came between 1808 and 1810; this difference may partially account for South Carolina's growing concern with the world situation during that period, for attitudes which varied from passive endurance to active belligerence. The South Carolina legislature in June, 1808, had expressed its willingness to enforce the embargo, but in reporting the resolutions to Jefferson, Speaker Joseph Alston did tell the President that they represented a wholehearted patriotism, not necessarily a "perfect unanimity of political opinion."[26] As economic conditions became tighter, there was growing resistance to the embargo and to its successor, nonintercourse.

Calhoun's public speech against the embargo in 1808 has already been cited. Governor Charles Pinckney in December, 1807, blamed disputes with Great Britain for "an almost total stagnation of commerce and stoppage of the sale of produce"; this caused "the great inconvenience of merchants and planters."[27] Fear that the international situation would bring the loss of markets gave impetus to such news stories as that which noted the phenomenal growth of South American cotton sales in Liverpool. By June, 1812, there were reports that cotton planters had been forced to turn to corn, that some upcountry men were turning to wheat.[28]

The situation in Charleston is well mirrored in the letters of Margaret Izard Manigault to her mother: cotton prices of 1811 were down to eight cents; money in town was almost nonexistent; and worst of all, since early 1809 there had scarcely been a party.[29]

South Carolina depended on unrestricted trade—on "commerce" as British minister Foster called it—because this was a region where people cultivated the soil, sold most of what they produced, and purchased most of what they consumed. Although the nonimportation law which succeeded the embargo in 1809 was often unenforced, general economic conditions kept on the downgrade as long as there was a controversy with England, the chief purchaser and provider in the South.[30] By the time of the Twelfth Congress, the tone of the South Carolina legislature had changed notably from that of 1808. This group sent resolutions to President Madison demanding that definite action be taken to protect commerce and the honor of the

---

[24] *Ibid.*, II, 45.
[25] MS Notes. Foster Papers.
[26] Note Wade Hampton's letter of April, 1808, and other comments in Wolfe, *Jeffersonian Democracy*, pp. 222–25.

[27] Charleston *Courier*, Dec. 2, 1807.
[28] *Ibid.*, Sept. 26, 1809; June 2, July 3, 1812.
[29] Margaret I. Manigault to Alice Izard, February, 1809, Dec. 1, 1811, Ralph Izard Papers, II, III, Library of Congress.
[30] Wolfe, *Jeffersonian Democracy*, p. 236; *Niles' Weekly Register*, I, 133. Incidentally, Great Britain received 60 per cent of the American cotton exports in 1811. Hammond, *Cotton Industry*, p. 358.

nation. A firm stand from the beginning, it was explained, might have prevented much loss to agriculture. D. R. Williams vigorously expressed the sentiments of his state before Congress:

But what is the condition of the commerce with Great Britain. . . . Truly miserable. . . . How is tobacco affected? . . . Inquire into the state of the cotton market; where is the crop of 1810? A curse to him who meddled with it. Where is that of 1811? Rotting at home in the hands of the grower, waiting the repeal of the Orders in Council.[31]

South Carolina had developed a decided urge for war. Excited by considerations of her primary livelihood, the export trade in cotton, South Carolina became one of the main protagonists of the conflict. This was not the largest or wealthiest state in the union, but it had one special qualification for national leadership in 1812—the most at stake in the domestic export trade; South Carolina had more exports per individual white person than any other state in the union. With only 3.6 per cent of the total white population of the United States, South Carolina exported 10.3 per cent of the domestic goods.[32] Whether or not fighting a war with England was the logical step to take as a remedy to the com-

mercial and thus agricultural distress is not the question—the South Carolinians of 1812 were convinced that a war would help.

To assess the total internal and external forces which produced the War of 1812 will call for the investigation of a multitude of factors not yet understood. The effort in this paper has been primarily to set forth the position of South Carolina with regard to the war, thereby pointing out in particular the significant part played by the direct trade of the United States, by foreign markets for staple products, in determining the course of events.

In the realm of international diplomacy, A. L. Burt's study goes farther than any other in explaining how the United States, entangled with both Great Britain and France, finally chose war with Britain. Burt's suggestions regarding the attitudes of the various sections of the United States toward going to war are also well directed. Making note of the fact that the South was sorely pinched for markets (and South Carolina indeed received considerable support in her war effort from Georgia, Virginia, and North Carolina), Burt further points out that the Northeast was "betraying national honor . . . for selfish profit." All sources indicate in fact that New England experienced a great shipping and commercial boom because of continuing European hostilities; the United States government went to war to "champion maritime interests . . . in spite of their opposition."[33] Burt's observations, apparently sound, are directly supported by the conclusion

---

[31] Speech of Jan. 6, 1812, *Annals*, p. 686. See also speech of Governor Henry Middleton giving a justification for war. *Niles' Weekly Register*, III, 275–76.

[32] *Ibid.*, I, 237, for figures from the Census of 1810; I, 399, for exports, domestic and foreign, for each state in 1811. South Carolina had 214,196 white population of the total 5,905,782 whites in the United States. (Counting the slave population full value, South Carolina had 5.8 per cent of the total.) South Carolina's domestic exports were valued at $4,650,934, while the total was $45,294,043. Maryland came close to South Carolina in trade per individual; with 3.9 per cent of the white population, her domestic trade was 10 per cent. However, she also had over 14 per cent of the total shipping trade, a factor which would greatly complicate her attitude toward war.

[33] A. L. Burt, *The United States, Great Britain, and British North America* (New Haven, 1940), p. 306. Burt explains that Great Britain, in command of the sea, pressed harder on American neutrality than France, which had no foothold on the American continent and therefore was less vulnerable.

of this paper that South Carolina, which played a significant role in the congressional campaign for war, had as its primary concern an alleviation of commercial distress.

The thesis of Julius W. Pratt, on the other hand, seems considerably weakened by the findings here reported. The coupling together of the South and Southwest in interpreting the war sentiment is certainly justifiable, but this alliance was not altogether natural, and in many respects the relationships that have been singled out are not the significant ones. Indian troubles may have had some bearing on western sentiment, but these did not pose a serious problem in the South at this date; expansion into Florida was likewise an unimportant urge.[34] The devel-

oping political philosophy of Kentucky and Tennessee could rarely be equated with that of conservative cotton-producing South Carolina, nor was the latter by 1812 in a position to share the frontier sentiments of the West. Indeed, the support of these states for similar measures in Congress lasted only a few years.

The significant basis of alliance between the South and the Southwest in 1812 was their common cry against foreign depredations on American shipping. As well-explained by G. R. Taylor, when depression replaced the early western prosperity in 1808 and 1809, discontent was rampant and settlers looked madly about them for the causes of their troubles. Economic analysts believe today that these were primarily difficulties within the frontier area itself—matters of transportation, communication, imperfect marketing, and insufficient financial organization. However, the westerners of 1808–1812 grasped for a time at the first likely cause; they began to be painfully aware of foreign restrictions on American commerce, and to these they directed more and more blame for their economic ills. Although western markets were actu-

---

[34] Warren H. Goodman, taking issue with Pratt's thesis, grants that Pratt had sufficient evidence to justify listing the Indians as a definite problem, but not as an "overmastering" concern. In line with Goodman's statement on the Indian question, if sample data from middle Tennessee in this writer's files are of value, there seems to have been no particular concern with Indians or any other British-inspired difficulties in the Williamson County frontier settlement in the years before 1812; see Williamson County MS Records, 1800–1812, Court House, Franklin, Tennessee. It is also interesting to note from a slightly different angle that Ohio, which was closer to the British-Indian sphere of influence than Kentucky and Tennessee, cast one vote for war in the House yet one against war in the Senate, the negative vote being given by Senator Thomas Worthington, a future governor of the state. See DAB, XX. Pratt's contention that the southern desire for war was a part of its acquisitive impulse toward Florida is weak. No evidence can be found in congressional debates that Florida was a motive for war. Actually, part of Florida was taken without a thought of conflict with Britain, and in June, 1812, a move by the House of Representatives to permit the occupation of East and West Florida was blocked by the Senate (Annals, pp. 1684–92). The Florida thesis can certainly not be applied in any sizable measure to South Carolina; Thomas Sumter had opposed even the purchase of Florida in 1806 because too large a portion of seacoast would be left undefended. (Everett S. Brown, ed., William Plumer's Memorandum of Proceedings in the United States Senate, 1803–1807 [New York, 1923], p. 421.) In November, 1812, William Lowndes expressed the opinion that no law would be recommended for the occupation of Florida because Spain was likely to cede it anyway. (Lowndes to [Thomas Pinckney], Nov. 27, 1812. William Lowndes Papers, Library of Congress.) There was certain agitation in Georgia over the question of Florida because of the common boundary, but it seems unwise to visualize the entire South as an expansive-minded area. The contention that a sectional bargain was made between North and South regarding the acquisition of Canada and Florida has been left completely without basis by W. H. Goodman, who has pointed out that the conquest of Canada was openly advocated in the South as early as 1807, no particular opposition to this move being voiced thereafter. Canada was often regarded in many parts of the country as possible remuneration for British damages to American commerce. See Goodman, "Origins of the War of 1812," pp. 177–82.

ally far less directly connected to European trade than those of South Carolina, increased demands for western hemp, tobacco, cotton, and flour were hopefully anticipated as results of a war with Great Britain. In 1812, "the right of exporting the productions of our own soil and industry to foreign markets" seemed as real to the hemp and tobacco growers of Kentucky as to the large-scale cotton producers of South Carolina.[35]

The internal scene in South Carolina was ripe for a burst of political activity on behalf of commerce. Contrary to the impression left by authors who have elected to discuss in isolation the rise of the Republican majority in South Carolina, the state's over-all outlook was largely a conservative one based on an established political and economic philosophy. The South Carolina Republican party itself could only in a superficial sense be described as Jeffersonian; more specifically it was a state-centered group which kept well in line with the prevailing statewide views, these marked by ambition for gain yet an innate distrust of substantial change. Such conservatism, prompted by the immediate need to preserve the prosperous economic system of the state, was expressed by South Carolina in a nationalistic impulse for war.

[35] The quotation is from a speech by Felix Grundy of Tennessee in which he singled out this right as the "true question in controversy." *Annals*, p. 424.

In a sense the war marked the end of one era of Jeffersonianism and the beginning of a change in the nature of the Republican party. South Carolina, one of the foremost war-minded leaders, was a state whose Republicanism had never been more than an independent, local movement. The new generation in the Republican party, with an aim to protect and promote the direct commerce of the country that seemed more Federalist than Jeffersonian, was strongly spearheaded by men from the South and the Southwest who worked together successfully in a congressional drive for war. The effective leadership of Henry Clay in the Speaker's chair supplemented by other representatives of the frontier regions must never be minimized, but that provides matter for another paper. Working with Clay, the new delegation from South Carolina was the most aggressive force in Congress.

Paradoxical as it may seem, the desire of South Carolina to preserve and extend the status quo produced a determination not to be undone by the caprices of warring European powers. Going to Congress with the conviction that the older Republican measures would not solve the problems of 1812, South Carolina's young Congressmen Calhoun, Cheves, and Lowndes spoke for the protection of America's foreign commerce and not at all incidentally for the well-being of South Carolina's trade in cotton.

Norman K. Risjord: 1812: CONSERVATIVES, WAR HAWKS, AND THE NATION'S HONOR

THE modern tendency to seek materialistic motives and economic factors in all human relations has greatly obscured one of the basic causes of the War of 1812. A generation of historians, brought up on the disillusionment that

From Norman K. Risjord, *William and Mary Quarterly*, XVIII (Apr. 1961), 196–210. Reprinted with permission.

followed the failure of the attempt to "make the world safe for democracy" in 1919, has persistently searched for the hidden economic factors behind all wars. Yet a cursory glance at the statistics of American commerce in the first decade of the nineteenth century will show that the War of 1812 was the most uneconomic war the United States has ever fought. A casual search through the letters and speeches of contemporaries reveals that those who fought the war were primarily concerned with the honor and integrity of the nation.

Students of the period are familiar with the standard explanation for the war: the election of 1810, by providing 63 new faces in a House of 142, represented a popular disillusionment with the Jeffersonian system and supplied the new Twelfth Congress with a number of young war hawks, such as Henry Clay, John C. Calhoun, and Felix Grundy, who were determined to assert America's position in the world. Since the loudest demand for strong measures, as well as some of the ablest of the war hawks, came from the West, historians have been channeled into a search for reasons why the West should have demanded a war for "free trade and sailors' rights"; the historiography of the period has been almost exclusively concerned with "Western war aims." The desire for land, Canadian or Indian, fear of a British-backed Indian conspiracy, concern over the declining prices of agricultural products and the restriction of markets abroad—all at one time or another have been represented as basic causes of the war.[1]

The weakness in this interpretation is that it virtually ignores the vote on the declaration of war in June 1812. The West may have been influenced by economic as well as patriotic motives, but the West, after all, had only ten votes in the House of Representatives. The South Atlantic states from Maryland to Georgia cast thirty-nine, or nearly half, of the seventy-nine votes for war in 1812. Any explanation of the war must place primary emphasis on the Southern Congressmen, and neither feature of the standard interpretation—the concept of a "revolution" in popular sentiment in 1810 and the emphasis on economic factors—satisfactorily explains their votes for war.

Most of these Southern Congressmen were "old Republicans," conservatives whose political Bible was the Republican platform of 1800 and who had sat in Congress for years. In the South there is no evidence of a sudden popular demand in the election of 1810 for a more energetic government and a more vigorous foreign policy. Maryland, which voted six to three for war in June 1812, had four new members in the Twelfth Congress, one a Federalist. The three new Republicans either won the election without opposition or they replaced men who had supported military preparations and a stronger foreign policy in the Eleventh Congress.[2]

---

[1] Warren H. Goodman, "The Origins of the War of 1812: A Survey of Changing Interpretations," *Mississippi Valley Historical Review*, XXVII (1941), 171–186, has a good discussion of the historiography of the causes of the war. The article was written before the latest interpretation in terms of neutral rights and impressments was published: Alfred L. Burt, *The United States, Great Britain, and British North America from the Revolution to the Establishment of Peace after the War of 1812* (New Haven, 1940). The most important recent contributions to the economic interpretation are Margaret Kinard Latimer, "South Carolina—A Protagonist of the War of 1812," *American Historical Review*, LXI (1955–56), 914–929, and Reginald Horsman, "Western War Aims, 1811–1812," *Indiana Magazine of History*, LII (1957), 1–16.

[2] *National Intelligencer* (Washington), Oct. 5, 8, 12, 1810. Maryland's three new Republicans were Joseph Kent of Bladensburg, Peter Little of

Virginia, which held her elections for the Twelfth Congress in the spring of 1811, returned a virtually identical delegation of seventeen Republicans and five Federalists. The two Quids, John Randolph and Edwin Gray, were re-elected, as were most of the conservative Republicans of the Eleventh Congress. The Shenandoah Valley remained as solidly Federalist as it had been in 1800, and the tramontane region, the one part of the state that might have been concerned with Indians and Western lands, elected Thomas Wilson, its first Federalist since 1793.

Virginia's election as a whole produced five new Republican members; none apparently was elected on the issue of peace or war. John Wayles Eppes, the only strong leader Virginia had sent to the Eleventh Congress, moved to John Randolph's district in the Southside and was defeated by Randolph in the election. The contest was close even though Eppes never formally declared himself a candidate, but the objections to Randolph centered on his vigorous opposition to the Madison administration. No one maintained that the election of Eppes would ensure stronger measures toward Great Britain.[3] Eppes's seat in his former district was taken by James Pleasants, a war Republican who in the postwar period was to revert to the old Jeffersonian strict-constructionist doctrines. In Thomas Jefferson's own district, which included Albemarle County, David S. Garland was replaced by Hugh Nelson,

a close friend of James Monroe and member of the "minority" that had supported Monroe against James Madison's election in 1808 because it felt that Madison was too nationalistic. Nelson entered the Twelfth Congress with a decided preference for peace at any price. In the Fredericksburg area the administration regular, Walter Jones, declined to run again, and in the election Major John P. Hungerford defeated John Taliaferro by six votes. Hungerford was a former Quid and had sat on the Monroe electoral committee in 1808. Taliaferro contested the election, received the support of the war hawks in the House, and was awarded the seat. In the Fauquier-Culpeper district John Love, who had generally supported preparedness measures in the Eleventh Congress, declined re-election and was replaced by another war Republican, Dr. Aylet Hawes.[4]

Nearly half the Virginia Congressmen were elected without opposition, and even where there was a contest the election seldom turned on the issue of foreign policy. Typical of Virginia conservatives re-elected in 1811 was John Clopton, who had represented the Richmond district since 1801. If a letter to his constituents published in the *Virginia Argus* is a fair summary of his campaign platform, Clopton was running in support of the nonintercourse law and against the Bank of the United States, giving no indication of any departure from the Jeffersonian system. Clopton had two opponents, one of whom withdrew before the election, while the other made public statements agreeing with Clopton on every issue.[5]

The election of 1810 in North Carolina similarly produced no great change in her

Baltimore, and Stephenson Archer of the Eastern Shore. They replaced Nicholas R. Moore, member of the war party in the 11th Congress, Archibald Van Horne, who had generally supported stronger measures, and John Montgomery, who had resigned his seat after being re-elected to the 12th Congress.

[3] See "Corvus," *Virginia Argus* (Richmond), Jan. 29, 1811.

[4] *Enquirer* (Richmond), Apr. 26, 30, May 3, 10, 1811.

[5] *Virginia Argus*, Mar. 28, Apr. 4, 1811, *Enquirer*, Mar. 26, Apr. 2, 1811.

representation. Of her twelve Congressmen eight were re-elected, two of them
Federalists and one, Richard Stanford, a
Randolph Quid. Two of the four new-
comers had served in Congress during
the Jefferson administration (William
Blackledge from 1803 to 1808 and
Thomas Blount from 1804 to 1808). The
only new faces in the North Carolina
group, Israel Pickens and William R.
King, were war hawks, but neither defeated an incumbent.[6]

The political "revolution" in South
Carolina in the election of 1810, which
produced a unanimous vote for war in
June 1812, was more apparent than real.
The election of the three great war hawk
leaders, John C. Calhoun, William
Lowndes, and Langdon Cheves, was
more an addition of talent than of numbers to the war party in Congress. In the
campaign Calhoun had openly advocated
war, but he was elected without opposition since the incumbent—his cousin Joseph Calhoun, a war hawk in the
Eleventh Congress—declined re-election
and supported him.[7] William Lowndes
succeeded to the seat of John Taylor, one
of the administration's floor leaders in the
Eleventh Congress who had been elected
to the Senate. Cheves was elected in 1810
to fill a vacant seat in the Eleventh Congress and was re-elected to the Twelfth.

The other prominent war hawk, David Rogerson Williams, took the seat of
his brother-in-law Robert Witherspoon,
who declined re-election and threw his
support to Williams.[8] Williams, moreover, as a member of the Ninth Congress,

had followed John Randolph in rebellion
against the Jefferson administration in
1806 and thus fits more into the pattern
of the converted conservative. Indeed, as
late as May 1812 a Federalist member of
the House observed that Williams was
still trying to make up his mind between
peace and war.[9] The only real contest in
South Carolina was the defeat of Lemuel
J. Alston by Elias Earle, but no current
issue was involved for the two men had
taken turns defeating each other for
years.[10]

The election in South Carolina illus-
trates the real significance of the election
of 1810. Without any fundamental
change in public opinion, and partly by
coincidence, South Carolina produced
some of the outstanding leaders of the
Twelfth Congress. But the change, as in
the Western elections that produced
Henry Clay and Felix Grundy, was primarily in ability rather than in numbers.
Indeed, speaking strictly in terms of numbers, the actual war hawks elected in
1810 were outvoted by Federalists and
antiwar Republicans in the Twelfth Congress. The young war hawks from the
South and West were certainly able men,
and largely by force of character alone
they led an unwilling and apathetic country to war.

Yet was leadership alone enough?
Several prominent war hawks—Clay,

[9] Samuel Taggart to Rev. John Taylor, May 9,
1812, "Letters of Samuel Taggart," American
Antiquarian Society, Proceedings, New Ser.,
XXXIII (Worcester, 1923), 399.
[10] John Harold Wolfe, Jeffersonian Democracy
in South Carolina, in James Sprunt Studies in
Historical and Political Science, XXIV (Chapel
Hill, 1940), 241, expresses a similar interpretation of the election in South Carolina; and Latimer, "South Carolina—A Protagonist of the War
of 1812," 916, though she emphasizes the economic factors in South Carolina, does not contest
this interpretation of the election.

[6] Star (Raleigh), Aug. 16, 23, 1810; Delbert H.
Gilpatrick, Jeffersonian Democracy in North
Carolina (New York, 1931), 241–244.
[7] Charles Wiltse, John C. Calhoun, Nationalist
(Indianapolis and New York, 1944), 51.
[8] Harvey T. Cook, The Life and Legacy of David
Rogerson Williams (New York, 1916), 84.

Richard M. Johnson, Ezekiel Bacon, Cheves, and Peter B. Porter—were members of the Eleventh Congress, but despite their ability they had been unable to lead that body in any consistent direction. At least as significant as the sudden appearance of a few talented war hawks in the Twelfth Congress was the gradual conversion of the average Republican from Jeffersonian pacifism to a vigorous defense of America's neutral rights. It was these men, most of them Southerners who had been in Congress for years, who provided the necessary votes for war, just as they had provided the main support for the embargo and nonintercourse laws. Their conversion seems to have stemmed primarily from a disillusionment with the old system of commercial retaliation and a growing realization that the only alternative to war was submission and national disgrace. Every expedient to avoid war honorably had been tried without success. Submission to the orders in council presaged a return to colonial status; war seemed the only alternative. The war, at least as far as the South was concerned, was brought on by men who had had a "bellyful" of England, not by men who were interested in Western lands, or Indians, or prices in the lower Mississippi Valley.

The major weakness in the various economic interpretations is their failure to explain the demand for war in the Middle Atlantic states and in the South. The "expansionist" school of historians, with internal variations, generally maintains that the war was the result of the Western desire for land, in Canada as well as in Indian-dominated Indiana, and that the conquest of Canada was demanded both for its own sake and because the British were backing the Te-

cumseh confederacy.[11] The difficulty is that the areas most concerned with these problems—Indiana, Illinois, and Michigan—were territories with no vote in Congress. Even Ohio, which presumably had a direct interest in the Wabash lands, was by no means unanimously in favor of war. Its one representative, Jeremiah Morrow, voted for war in 1812 just as he had voted for the embargo in 1807, but Ohio's two senators, Thomas Worthington and Alexander Campbell, opposed war in 1812 because the nation was unprepared and they feared an Indian attack on the defenseless frontier. Both preferred to retain the old system of commercial retaliation.[12] Some have suggested that Ohio's senators were out of touch with public sentiment, but a recent biographer of Worthington feels that a plebiscite held in the spring of 1812 would probably have shown a majority of the people of Ohio against war.[13] Kentucky and Tennessee, it is true, showed considerable interest in the Indian lands and in Canada, but even so their votes in Congress were hardly enough to carry the country to war.

Julius W. Pratt, leading proponent of the "expansionist" thesis, circumvented this difficulty by conjecturing a "frontier crescent" of war hawks extending from New Hampshire (John A. Harper) to Kentucky (Clay and Johnson) and Tennessee (Felix Grundy) and ending in

[11] Louis M. Hacker, "Western Land Hunger and the War of 1812: A Conjecture," *Miss. Valley Hist. Rev.*, X (1923–24), 365–395; Julius W. Pratt, *Expansionists of 1812* (New York, 1925), 12–14; Pratt, "Western War Aims in the War of 1812," *Miss. Valley Hist. Rev.*, XII (1925–26), 36–50.

[12] Diary of Thomas Worthington, June 14, 17, 1812, Library of Congress, Washington, D.C.

[13] Alfred Byron Sears, *Thomas Worthington* (Columbus, 1958), 175. Nearly all reviewers have questioned this assertion, but Sears is certainly right in assuming that opinion was divided.

South Carolina (Calhoun, Lowndes, and Cheves) and Georgia (George M. Troup.)[14] Yet this seems an arbitrary conjunction of dissimilar areas. Why should New Hampshire or Vermont have been interested enough in the Wabash lands to go to war? And how explain a Southern interest in the Wabash or in Canada? Pratt plugged this hole by surmising a bargain between Southern and Western war hawks in which Florida would be brought into the Union to balance the conquest of Canada. The only evidence he cites, however, is one editorial in a Tennessee newspaper.[15]

It is true that Southern war hawks talked much about the conquest of Canada, but they seem to have regarded it as primarily a method of conducting the war rather than as an ultimate objective. Secretary of State Monroe, for instance, felt that Canada might be invaded, "not as an object of the war but as a means to bring it to a satisfactory conclusion."[16] On the other hand there is evidence that some Southerners actually feared the annexation of Canada. John Randolph certainly considered the possibility that Canada might be acquired the best of reasons for not going to war, and a fellow Virginian elected in 1810 wrote home in December 1811: "The New Yorkers and Vermonters are very well inclined to have upper Canada united with them, by way of increasing their influence in the Union."[17] As to the other half of the bar-

gain there is little evidence that outside of the border area the South was much interested in Florida, and recent scholars have tended to minimize the importance of Florida in the Southern demand for war.[18]

Somewhat more plausible is the economic interpretation of the war in terms of declining farm prices and the restriction of markets abroad. This point of view was first put forth in the early 1930's by George Rogers Taylor, who suggested that the declining price of agricultural products, particularly in the lower Mississippi Valley, may have been a factor in the Western demand for war. The gist of this argument is summed up in a letter of a Louisiana planter of July 25, 1811: "Upon the subject of cotton we are not such fools, but we know that . . . the British are giving us what they please for it. . . . But we happen to know that we should get a much greater price for it, for we have some idea of the extent of the Continent, and the demand there for it; . . . and, therefore, upon the score of lucre, as well as national honor, we are ready."[19] More recently, this argument has been adopted to explain the West-South alliance. Both sections were concerned with the declining prices of the great staple exports, cotton, tobacco, and hemp, and were inclined to blame the British orders in council for restricting

[14] Pratt, Expansionists of 1812, 126–127.
[15] Ibid.; Pratt, "Western War Aims in the War of 1812," 36–50.
[16] Monroe, The Writings of James Monroe . . . , ed. Stanislaus Murray Hamilton, V (New York, 1901), 207; see also, Marguerite B. Hamer, "John Rhea of Tennessee," East Tennessee Historical Society, Publications, No. 4 (Knoxville, 1932), 39.
[17] Hugh Nelson to Dr. Charles Everette, Dec. 22, 1811, Hugh Nelson Papers, Library of Congress, Washington, D.C.

[18] Burt, United States, Great Britain, and British North America, 306; Horsman, "Western War Aims, 1811–1812," 15; Weymouth T. Jordan, George Washington Campbell of Tennessee, in Florida State University Studies, No. 17 (Tallahassee, 1955), 94; Latimer, "South Carolina—A Protagonist of the War of 1812," 927.
[19] George R. Taylor, "Agrarian Discontent in the Mississippi Valley Preceding the War of 1812," Journal of Political Economy, XXXIX (1931), 499–500; see also, Taylor, "Prices in the Mississippi Valley Preceding the War of 1812," Journal of Economic and Business History, III (1930), 148–163.

their markets. The South and West, in this view, went to war primarily to defend the right to export their products without interference from Britain.[20]

That prices for these great staples declined gradually throughout the first decade of the century cannot be denied, but to what extent the British blockades were responsible is more difficult to determine. The direct trade in agricultural products was not generally affected by the orders in council; not till the winter of 1811–12 did the British interfere with cotton shipments, though their action at that time helped to justify war—at least in the mind of the North Carolina planter Nathaniel Macon.[21] It is interesting, however, that despite the British orders the market for cotton was rapidly increasing both in quantity exported and in geographical area. The declining price was a long-term phenomenon only temporarily interrupted by the postwar prosperity, rather than a result of British restrictions. Statistics on the export of tobacco similarly give no real indication that the British orders in council were responsible for the constriction in markets or the drop in prices.[22]

It is true, however, that the opinion that British restrictions were responsible for lower prices, even if unjustified, seems to have been widely held in the South. Margaret Kinard Latimer has recently brought to light evidence that this was a major factor in the demand for war at least in South Carolina. "Whether or not

fighting a war with England," she concludes, "was the logical step to take as a remedy to the commercial and thus agricultural distress is not the question—the South Carolinians of 1812 were convinced that a war would help."[23] Yet this leaves unanswered the question of why South Carolinians preferred to ignore the probability that war would further disrupt their commerce, while others, notably the New Englanders, were so painfully aware of it. Is it possible that those South Carolina politicians who stressed the cotton depression as a cause for war were merely supplying additional reasons that might influence the wavering?

It must also be remembered that the decline in prices was not universal. Prices for beef, corn, and flour, the main exports of the Middle Atlantic states, actually increased over the decade, while the price of pork declined only slightly. In 1810–11 total exports in these products nearly doubled as American farms fed the Duke of Wellington's army in Spain.[24] Pennsylvania, which voted sixteen to two for war with England, can hardly have been following the dictates of economic interest.

The South and the Middle Atlantic states, whose Congressmen furnished the major support for war, had little to gain economically from the conflict. Their direct trade in agricultural products was scarcely affected by the orders in council, and England had long been the major foreign market for both sections. Indeed, it might even be argued that these sections stood to lose as much by war as did New England. When, therefore, Nathaniel Macon spoke of going to war "to obtain the privilege of carrying the produce of our lands to a market"—an oft-quoted

[20] Horsman, "Western War Aims, 1811–1812," 9; Latimer, "South Carolina—A Protagonist of the War of 1812," 924–929.
[21] U. S., Congress, *The Debates and Proceedings in the Congress of the United States . . . ,* 12th Congress, 1st session, XXIII (Washington, 1853), 492–495; hereafter cited as *Annals of Congress.*
[22] Timothy Pitkin, *A Statistical View of the Commerce of the United States of America* (New Haven, 1935), 131–132, 134–137.

[23] Latimer, "South Carolina—A Protagonist of the War of 1812," 926.
[24] Pitkin, *Statistical View,* 96, 105, 119–120, 125–126, 128–129.

passage—he undoubtedly had in mind the "privilege" as much as the trade.[25] Southerners went to war primarily to defend their rights, not their purses.

This is not to deny that economic factors were present. The final synthesis of the causes of the war will have to take into account various material factors—the fear of an Indian conspiracy in the West, for instance, and the concern over declining prices in the South—but it will also have to recognize that none of these economic theses furnishes a satisfactory explanation for the general demand for war. The only unifying factor, present in all sections of the country, was the growing feeling of patriotism, the realization that something must be done to vindicate the national honor. In recent years historians have tended more and more to stress this factor, particularly in its influence on the West, where a feeling of national pride was an obvious concomitant of the youth and exuberance of that section.[26] Even Julius W. Pratt admitted that the war fever in the West "was doubtless due to various causes—perhaps most of all to sheer exasperation at the long continued dilatory fashion of handling the nation's foreign affairs."[27] This factor was probably even more important in the Middle Atlantic states and in the South where fewer material interests were at stake.

The system of commercial retaliation itself had not been defended on economic grounds. The first nonintercourse resolution had been introduced in the spring of 1806 by a Pennsylvanian, Andrew Gregg,

as an instrument for gaining by peaceful means some recognition of America's neutral rights. The embargo and the later nonintercourse laws were intended to furnish the President with a lever of negotiation, to maintain the national dignity short of war. It was the growing disillusionment with this system, the growing feeling that war was the only means for maintaining the nation's integrity that eventually brought on the conflict. This mental conversion is aptly illustrated by the following letter of John Clopton of Virginia.

Let us consider what our government has done—how long it has borne with the repeated injuries which have been touched on in this letter—how often negotiations have been resorted to for the purpose of avoiding war; and the aggressions, instead of having been in any measure relaxed have been pursued with aggravating violence without a single ray of expectation that there exists any sort of disposition in the B[ritish] Cabinet to relax, but the strongest disposition to persist in their career.

. . . The outrages in impressing American seamen exceed all manner of description. Indeed the whole system of aggression now is such that the real question between G. Britain and the U. States has ceased to be a question merely relating to certain rights of commerce about which speculative politicians might differ in opinion—it is now clearly, positively, and directly *a question of independence*, that is to say, whether the U. States are really an independent nation.[28]

Not all Republicans came to a similar conclusion at the same time. The process was a gradual one, beginning with the

[25] *Annals of Congress*, 12th Cong., 1st sess., XXIII, 663.
[26] Bernard Mayo, *Henry Clay* (Boston, 1937), 326–334; Burt, *United States, Great Britain, and British North America*, 306ff.; Horsman, "Western War Aims, 1811–1812," 1–18 passim.
[27] Pratt, *Expansionists of 1812*, 42.

[28] To (?), Apr. 20, 1812, John Clopton Papers, Duke University Library, Durham, North Carolina.

Chesapeake affair and the failure of the embargo to secure a recognition of American rights. The prominent Virginia Republican, Wilson Cary Nicholas, was one of the first to conclude that war was inevitable. Shortly after the Randolph schism in 1806, Nicholas had entered Congress at the behest of Jefferson, who needed an able floor leader in the House. The failure of the embargo convinced him that the whole policy of commercial retaliation was unsound, for it could not be enforced effectively enough to coerce the belligerents and it resulted only in the ruin of American agriculture. Since the Madison administration was unwilling to abandon the policy, Nicholas, rather than go into opposition, resigned his seat in the autumn of 1809.[29] "We have tried negotiation until it is disgraceful to think of renewing it," he wrote Jefferson. "Commercial restrictions have been so managed as to operate only to our own injury. War then or submission only remain. In deciding between them I cannot hesitate a moment."[30] George Washington Campbell of Tennessee reached a similar conclusion shortly after the *Chesapeake* affair, and he became one of the leading advocates for military preparations in the Tenth and Eleventh Congresses.[31]

The gradual realization of the need for a more militant foreign policy was also reflected in the prominent Republican newspapers. Thomas Ritchie of the Richmond *Enquirer* considered the embargo the only honorable alternative to war, and when it was repealed Ritchie and the *Enquirer* began openly advocating

war with England.[32] William Duane, editor of the Philadelphia *Aurora*, generally supported the system of commercial retaliation, but the repudiation of David Erskine's agreement and the mission of Francis "Copenhagen" Jackson in the fall of 1809 convinced him that Britain did not intend to negotiate the question of neutral rights. By December 1809 he was advocating military preparations, the arming of American merchant ships, and, if those measures failed to intimidate Britain, "defensive war."[33]

The old Jeffersonian, Nathaniel Macon, struggled long and valiantly with his conscience in an effort to reconcile Republican dogma with the obvious need for a vigorous defense of American rights. Throughout the Eleventh Congress he had been one of the administration leaders in the House, yet his basic conservatism was frequently evident. In the spring of 1810 he co-operated with John Randolph's efforts to reduce the size of the army and navy, even advocating that they be abolished altogether.[34] As chair-

[29] *An Address from Wilson Cary Nicholas to His Constituents* (Richmond, 1809).
[30] Dec. 22, 1809, Carter-Smith Papers, University of Virginia Library, Charlottesville, Virginia.
[31] Jordan, *George Washington Campbell of Tennessee,* 66–67.

[32] Charles H. Ambler, *Thomas Ritchie* (Richmond, 1913), 45.
[33] *Aurora* (Philadelphia), Mar. 4, July 21, Dec. 14, 1809. Erskine, the British ambassador, had reached an agreement with President Madison in 1809, under which the orders in council would be withdrawn in exchange for suspension of the American nonintercourse acts. Erskine's instructions were to secure a suspension of the nonintercourse system as a prior condition to agreement, but he violated his instructions and Madison announced the suspension of the nonintercourse acts only as a consequence of the agreement. When word of the agreement reached London, George Canning repudiated it, recalled Erskine, and sent to the United States the notorious "Copenhagen" Jackson. Jackson arrived in Washington in August, refused to discuss either reparations for the *Chesapeake* or revision of the orders in council, and in November, Madison suspended all further communication with him.
[34] *Annals of Congress,* 11th Cong., 2d sess., XXI (Washington, 1853), 1863; see also, Macon to Nicholson, Apr. 3, 1810, Joseph H. Nicholson Papers, Library of Congress, Washington, D.C.

man of the foreign relations committee, Macon reported the nonintercourse bill of April 1810, known as Macon's Bill Number Two, but he personally opposed it because he felt it too provocative.[35] Not until the beginning of the Twelfth Congress did he reach the conclusion that war was the only alternative. War was justified, he told the House in December 1811, because of the recent British seizures of ships carrying American agricultural products. This new aggression, he felt, showed that the British, instead of becoming more lenient, were actually tightening their system, and that further negotiation was useless.[36] Macon thereafter co-operated with the war hawks but with some reluctance and with an occasional lapse. He voted against every effort to increase the size of the navy, and he consistently opposed all efforts during the session to raise the taxes to finance the war.

A number of Republicans, though they co-operated with the preparedness measures of the war hawks, could not make up their minds on the basic issue of peace or war until the last minute. As late as May 1812 a Massachusetts Federalist reported, perhaps somewhat wishfully, that a majority of the Virginia delegation was still against war. Besides the Federalists and the Quids, Randolph and Gray, he listed Taliaferro, Nelson, William A. Burwell, John Smith, and Matthew Clay as opposed to war.[37] Representative of this group was Hugh Nelson. Nelson had been elected in 1811, but entered the Twelfth Congress with a lingering sympathy for the old Republican

"minority" whose leader was John Randolph of Roanoke and whose prophet was John Taylor of Caroline. "I am a messmate of J[ohn] R[andolph]," he wrote to a friend in Charlottesville shortly after his arrival in Washington. "The more I see him the more I like him. He is as honest as the sun, with all his foibles, and as much traduced I believe as any man has ever been. . . . Do not be surprised if before the session closes I am classified with him as a minority man."[38] Nelson's maiden speech in the House came on the resolution to increase the size of the regular army. It was a rehash of all the old Republican antiwar arguments—war would centralize the government, strengthen the executive, burden the people with taxes, armies, and navies, undermine our "republican simplicity," and subvert the Constitution. "I care not for the prices of cotton and tobacco as compared with the Constitution," he averred. Moreover he felt it unlikely that the United States could ever gain recognition of her neutral rights, particularly since the only program the war hawks suggested was a territorial war begun by an invasion of Canada. Canada could not be conquered, but even if it could, would this enforce our rights? "Certainly not. The way to enforce these rights was by way of a great maritime force, which the nation were incompetent to raise and support." Nelson nevertheless felt the country should prepare for any eventuality because unless Britain relented there was no alternative to war. "I shall vote for the increase of the regular force," he concluded, "to go hand in hand with my friends, even in a war, if necessary and just."[39] The most important of these

[35] Macon to Nicholson, Apr. 3, 6, 10, 1810, Joseph H. Nicholson Papers.
[36] Annals of Congress, 12th Cong., 1st sess., XXIII, 492–495.
[37] Samuel Taggart to Rev. John Taylor, May 9, 1812, "Letters of Samuel Taggart," Amer. Antiq. Soc., Proc., XXXIII, 398.

[38] To Dr. Charles Everette, Dec. 4, 1811, Hugh Nelson Papers.
[39] Annals of Congress, 12th Cong., 1st sess., XXIII, 497–499.

friends was Nelson's neighbor from Charlottesville, Secretary of State Monroe, who by the spring of 1812 was a vigorous advocate of strong measures. In June, John Randolph wrote to John Taylor of Caroline that Monroe was "most furiously warlike & carries the real strength of the Southern representation with him."[40]

Even more important than the personal influence of Monroe was the stimulus provided by President Madison. Most of the conservatives considered themselves loyal Republicans and were accustomed to following Presidential leadership in dealing with Britain and France. The policy of commercial retaliation had been largely an administration measure, and when the Twelfth Congress assembled in November 1811 Congress naturally looked to the Executive for guidance. Madison not only encouraged the war fever but he co-operated with the war hawks to a degree that has only recently begun to be fully recognized. His Annual Message to Congress in November 1811 outlined a program of military and naval preparations that was adopted virtually intact by the war hawks.[41] His release of the correspondence of Captain John Henry in March 1812 and his request in April for a thirty-day embargo as a prelude to war have been interpreted by his most recent biographer, Irving Brant, as attempts to stimulate the war sentiment in Congress.[42]

The war hawks took full advantage of these moves by the President in their efforts to hold the conservatives in line. In the later stages of the session, when a number of Republicans began to get cold feet, the war hawks informed them that it was too late to back out. When in April the bill initiating a temporary embargo was reported for debate, Henry Clay warned the House that if it stopped now after all the war measures it had passed, it would cover itself "with shame and indelible disgrace."[43] That this argument was effective is indicated by John Smilie, who followed Clay on the floor. Smilie, whose western-Pennsylvania Republicanism dated back to the fight over the Constitution in 1787, admitted that from the beginning of the session he had only reluctantly voted for the various proposals of the war hawks. He actually preferred continuing commercial retaliation to a war and an army of 25,000. But he realized it was too late to back down now; the nation's honor was at stake: "If we now recede we shall be a reproach to all nations."[44]

Added to this internal stimulus was the pressure of continuing British intransigence. On May 22 dispatches arrived in Washington from British Foreign Secretary Lord Castlereagh that contained nothing but a restatement of the British position. President Madison himself concluded that this was the last formal notice intended by the British government and sent his war message to Congress on June 1. It is not difficult to conceive that many a reluctant Republican came to the same decision.

It was thus with mixed motives that a majority of Republicans followed the war hawks to war. It is nevertheless clear that

---

[40] June 16, 1812, John Taylor Papers, Massachusetts Historical Society, Boston, Mass.

[41] Irving Brant, *James Madison, the President, 1809–1812* (Indianapolis and New York, 1956), 357–358, 363, 391.

[42] *Ibid.*, 415, 429. Capt. Henry was a British secret agent who had reported to Governor Craig of Canada on the discontent in New England during the time of the embargo. In February 1812 Henry, through the agency of a French nobleman, Count Crillon, sold his evidence of the disaffection in New England to the American State Department for $50,000.

[43] *Annals of Congress*, 12th Cong., 1st sess., XXIV (Washington, 1853), 1588–89.

[44] *Ibid.*, 1593–94.

a primary factor in the mind of each was the conclusion that the only alternative to war was submission to the British commercial system. The balance of power in the House was held by men who had been in Congress for years, who had tried every expedient short of war to secure a recognition of American rights, and who at last had become surfeited with British commercial regulations. The war hawks, it is true, provided with their skill and energy the necessary impetus to war, but they could not have done so had not a majority of the Republican Party, particularly in the South, become gradually converted to the idea that war was the only alternative to national humiliation and disgrace. In this sense the war hawks acted as the intangible catalyst for a reaction whose basic elements were already present.

Suggestions for Additional Reading

Two excellent studies of the causes of the War of 1812 not represented in this volume are Warren H. Goodman, "The Origins of the War of 1812: A Survey of Changing Interpretations," *Mississippi Valley Historical Review,* XXVIII (Sept. 1941), 171–186 and, more recently, Reginald Horsman, "Western War Aims, 1811–1812," *Indiana Magazine of History,* LIII (March 1957), 1–18. Both provide a critical review of the literature. For a fuller statement of the points of view presented in these readings by A. L. Burt, Julius W. Pratt, and George Rogers Taylor, the student should refer to the original publications. These are cited in footnotes at the beginning of each selection. Pratt also defends his thesis in "Western War Aims in the War of 1812," *The Mississippi Valley Historical Review,* XII (June 1925), 36–50 and in a review of Burt's book in *The American Historical Review,* XLVII (Oct. 1941), 87–89.

In his article "Western Land Hunger and the War of 1812: A Conjecture," *Mississippi Valley Historical Review,* X (March 1924), 365–395, Louis M. Hacker suggests that an important motive for war was the desire of the westerners for more land. George Dangerfield, *The Era of Good Feelings* (London, 1953) stresses the importance of frontier imperialism as a cause of the war.

Two comprehensive, book-length studies have recently been published on the causes of the War of 1812: Bradford Perkins, *Prologue to War: England and The United States, 1805–1812* (Berkeley and Los Angeles, 1961) and Reginald Horsman, *The Causes of The War of 1812* (Philadelphia, 1962). Besides add-ing much that is new and revealing on the internal political situation in Great Britain as well as in the United States, both authors make a serious attempt to weigh the various factors involved in the coming of the war.

Of the semi-popular accounts of the coming of the war perhaps the best is Albert Z. Carr, *The Coming of the War, An Account of the Remarkable Events Leading to the War of 1812* (Garden City, New York, 1960). The story is told in briefer compass in Francis F. Beirne, *The War of 1812* (New York, 1949), Chapters 1–9.

Politics and diplomacy are emphasized in Henry Adams' classic work, *History of the United States of America.* Volumes V and VI (New York, 1890) cover the years 1809–1813. Books on diplomatic history such as Thomas A. Bailey, *A Diplomatic History of the American People* (4th ed., New York, 1950) and Samuel Flagg Bemis, *A Diplomatic History of the United States* (3rd ed., New York, 1953) provide good general accounts of the changing international situation.

Biographies have been written on a number of the leaders who took an active part in the events preceding the war. Among the most useful are Irving Brant, *James Madison, The President 1809–1812* (Indianapolis, 1956); Bernard Mayo, *Henry Clay, Spokesman of the New West* (Cambridge, Mass., 1937); and Charles M. Wiltse, *John C. Calhoun, Nationalist, 1782–1828* (New York, 1944).

The economic conditions during the years leading up to the war are covered in Walter B. Smith and Arthur H. Cole, *Fluctuations in American Business, 1790–*

1860 (Cambridge, 1935) and in two more recent books: Curtis P. Nettles, *The Emergence of a National Economy* (New York, 1962) and Douglass C. North, *The Economic Growth of the United States, 1790–1860* (Englewood Cliffs, N.J., 1961). For the record of price behavior during the pre-war years, as well as some analysis of economic conditions, Arthur H. Cole's *Wholesale Commodity Prices in the United States, 1700–1861* (Cambridge, 1938) and the *Statistical Supplement* to the foregoing work are indispensable. Also useful in this connection are Anne Bezanson et al., *Wholesale Prices in Philadelphia, 1784–1861* (Philadelphia, 1936); and Thomas Senior Berry, *Western Prices before 1861: A Study of the Cincinnati Market* (Cambridge, 1943).

The standard work on American foreign commerce is Emory R. Johnson and others, *History of Domestic and Foreign Commerce of the United States,* (2 vols., Washington, D.C., 1915). More specialized are Charles S. Hyneman, *The First American Neutrality* (Illinois Studies in the Social Sciences XX, Urbana, 1934) and Anna C. Clauder, *American Commerce as Affected by the Wars of the French Revolution and Napoleon, 1793–1812* (Philadelphia, 1932). Eli F. Heckscher's *The Continental System, an Economic Interpretation* (Oxford, 1922) provides an exhaustive study of the subject indicated.

Contemporary materials on the causes of the war and the events leading up to it are available in state papers, newspapers, the correspondence of the principals involved, and *The Annals of Congress.* Part of the readings in this volume have been taken from this last source, but the student will find much of further interest in the proceedings, not only of the Twelfth Congress, but also of the preceding ones.